YORK NOTES

T.S. Eliot
The Waste Land

Note by Alasdair D.F. Macrae

Longman   York Press

The right of Alasdair D.F. Macrae to be identified as Author of this Work has been asserted by her in accordance with the Copyright, Designs and Patents Act 1988

YORK PRESS
322 Old Brompton Road, London SW5 9JH

PEARSON EDUCATION LIMITED
Edinburgh Gate, Harlow,
Essex CM20 2JE, United Kingdom
Associated companies, branches and representatives throughout the world

First published 2001
Sixth impression 2008

ISBN: 978-0-582-42474-6

Designed by Vicki Pacey
Phototypeset by Gem Graphics, Trenance, Mawgan Porth, Cornwall
Colour reproduction and film output by Spectrum Colour
Produced by Pearson Education Asia Limited, Hong Kong

CONTENTS

PART ONE

INTRODUCTION

HOW TO STUDY A POEM

Studying on your own requires self-discipline and a carefully thought-out work plan in order to be effective.

- Poetry is the most challenging kind of literary writing. In your first reading you may well not understand what the poem is about. Don't jump too swiftly to any conclusions about the poem's meaning.
- Read the poem many times, and including out loud. After the second or third reading, write down any features you find interesting or unusual.
- What is the poem's tone of voice? What is the poem's mood?
- Does the poem have an argument? Is it descriptive?
- Is the poet writing in his or her own voice? Might he or she be using a **persona** or mask?
- Is there anything special about the kind of language the poet has chosen? Which words stand out? Why?
- What elements are repeated? Consider **alliteration, assonance, rhyme, rhythm, metaphor** and ideas.
- What might the poem's **images** suggest or symbolise?
- What might be significant about the way the poem is arranged in lines? Is there a regular pattern of lines? Does the grammar coincide with the ending of the lines or does it 'run over'? What is the effect of this?
- Do not consider the poem in isolation. Can you compare and contrast the poem with any other work by the same poet or with any other poem that deals with the same theme?
- What do you think the poem is about?
- Every argument you make about the poem must be backed up with details and quotations that explore its language and organisation.
- Always express your ideas in your own words.

This York Note offers an introduction to *The Waste Land* and cannot substitute for close reading of the text and the study of secondary sources

In the autumn of 1922, *The Waste Land* was published in London and New York. Earlier in the same year, James Joyce's *Ulysses* had been published. These two works, a poem and a novel, quickly came to be recognised as the central literary texts of **modernism** and their influence on subsequent literature across the world has been inestimable. Contemporary readers found *The Waste Land* baffling, challenging, exciting, innovative, disconcerting, in various proportions, and readers now still share many of these reactions. Eliot's poem retains its status as the most revolutionary poem in English since the shock caused by Wordsworth and Coleridge's publication of *Lyrical Ballads* in 1798–1800. After all the years that have passed, after all that has been written about it, *The Waste Land* has not settled into some comfortable niche. The poem remains difficult, both in its formal aspects and its ideas, and new readers have to grapple for themselves, with what help they can find, to get some firm hold on it. The awkwardness derives, in part, from the variegatedness through the poem but it is this very variegatedness that allows different readers to engage with, even on a first reading, attractive elements such as poignant, lyrical passages; surreally strange **imagery**; memorable lines; segments which are persuasive in their catching of a mood or an existential attitude; comic passages, even if the humour is rather grim.

The Waste Land forces readers to face difficult questions concerning values, related to religion, morality, history and art. Are values communal or individual? We, as readers, are addressed and interrogated by the poem and responses are demanded of us; the poem does not provide answers or solutions. Although it is very obviously a construction of its time and incorporated in itself contemporary developments in the visual arts, music and cinema as well as in literature, it continues to broadcast beyond its period of creation, beyond the twentieth century. No poet of any ambition since 1922 can afford to ignore *The Waste Land*, and no individual concerned with how to live a decent or significant life can ignore the challenge set by the poem.

C OMMENTARY

Towards the end of 1919, Eliot said in a letter to his mother that he was about to start on a long poem. During the years 1919–22 Eliot was overworked, his health was bad, his wife was mentally and physically ill, their marriage was painful to both of them, they were constantly short of money and the future looked bleak. Eliot could not find the time necessary to concentrate on a long poem but in the autumn of 1921 he was given leave from his job to visit a psychologist in Switzerland.

By January 1922, Eliot had handed over to Ezra Pound what he had written while abroad. The final poem as published in October 1922 was very markedly the result of the collaboration between the two poets. The main effects of Pound's suggestions were to tighten the organisation of the poem and to remove some overwritten satirical sketches and personal elements. Eliot was also advised by Pound against using his earlier poem *Gerontion* as a prelude to *The Waste Land*.

The notes, which now accompany the poem, were not part of Eliot's original plan and were not present with the first publication. When the New York publishing company, Boni and Liveright, accepted the poem for publication in book form, they asked Eliot to add some material to make up the size of a small book. Later in his life, Eliot came to regret the inclusion of the notes because he felt that they distracted readers' attention from the poem itself, but he did not have them removed.

When the poem was published Eliot presented the manuscripts and typescripts with his and Pound's revisions as a gift to John Quinn (1870–1924), a New York lawyer. On Quinn's death in 1924 the manuscripts disappeared, and speculation as to their contents and their fate continued until 1968, when they were discovered in the New York Public Library. Eliot's widow Valerie prepared a transcript of the original sheets; this was published by Faber in 1971.

This Note refers to *The Waste Land* published in *T.S. Eliot: The Waste Land and other poems* by Faber and Faber (1972). Quotations from the Bible are taken from the Holy Bible, Authorized King James Version, published by Collins (1953).

GENERAL SUMMARY

Except in the case of narrative poems, it is extremely difficult to summarise a poem in a way that is fair to the nature of the poem. Because of its organisation (see Critical Approaches: Structure), *The Waste Land* resists the very idea of a summary. Nonetheless, like any other object, it can be described and even a crude summary may help to indicate the general shape of the poem.

In Part I, 'The Burial of the Dead', Eliot conveys a sense of apprehension and incomprehension in various characters presented in different situations. The lack of understanding is not helped by Madame Sosostris, a fortune-teller, whose enigmatic pronouncements only make sense later in the poem. The city, in particular London, is a grim place of people unable to live fully or see a way out of their deadness.

Part II, 'A Game of Chess', offers two scenes showing the essential emptiness of people's lives. The first presents, in a lavishly decorated room, a rich lady whose constant questions express her anxiety and lack of control. The second scene is set in a London pub where two women discuss the predicament in which Lil finds herself.

The theme of sexual dissatisfaction is explored in Part III, 'The Fire Sermon', where Eliot, moving about in time from Buddha and St Augustine to the present day, shows how man's aspirations to a higher, more spiritual mode of living are constantly thwarted by his subservience to his bodily appetites and his self-centredness.

In the brief Part IV, 'Death by Water', a drowned merchant's body decomposes in the sea. The merchant seems to have achieved nothing.

Part V, 'What the Thunder said', begins with a description of the death of Jesus and goes on to relate a gruelling journey through the desert to an empty chapel. The traveller has to suffer hardships, delusions and a sense that all is chaotic and meaningless before he arrives. In the final section of the poem the arrival of rain is intimated and the voice of the thunder offers three words of advice: 'give', 'sympathise', and 'control'. At the very end these words are set alongside various phrases which echo themes and motifs which have appeared earlier in the poem.

If you are unfamiliar with *The Waste Land* or feel daunted by the prospect of reading the summaries and commentaries below, you may prefer to read Part Three, Critical Approaches, first. This discusses, among other things, the structure, language, style and meaning of *The Waste Land* and may give you an overview of the poem before focusing on the detail. Either way, this Note and the poem itself will benefit from being read on many occasions. Enjoy learning to understand this important work.

THE TITLE

Eliot, in his preliminary note to the poem, acknowledges his indebtedness to two works: *The Golden Bough* (1890–1915) by Sir James Frazer and *From Ritual to Romance* (1920) by Jessie L. Weston. The part of Frazer's work that particularly excited Eliot is concerned with the **myths** associated with Adonis, Osiris and Attis. These deities were seen by successive civilisations in the Eastern Mediterranean and the Middle East as the powers of nature and, each year, ceremonies were performed in their honour to ensure the return of spring and the fertility of the crops. Water is essential for fertility; without water, in rain or river, the land and the people die. Following Frazer, Jessie Weston showed that the rituals and myths associated with these deities did not die out on the arrival of Christianity but were incorporated into the material of literature in medieval Europe. In particular, she traced the legend of the Holy Grail in the chivalric romances. The Grail of the story was the cup used by Christ at his Last Supper with his disciples and later used to catch the dripping blood from his crucified body. It was believed that this sacred relic was brought to Glastonbury in England before being lost. The search for the lost Grail was symbolic of human search for truth. The questing knight of the romances had to journey to the Chapel Perilous and there learn to ask the right questions concerning the Grail and the Lance which had pierced Christ's side on the Cross.

The cup and spear also carry a sexual symbolism of the female and male elements necessary for regeneration. This overlapping of the spiritual and the physical is contained in the figure who lies behind the questing knight. The Fisher King is the sexually wounded ruler of a country which has itself become infertile and the search for the Grail is undertaken by his knight to restore life to his kingdom. Jessie Weston saw in the title, the Fisher King, a definite connection between the fish as representative of the basic water of all life and the fish symbol so closely associated with the early Christian Church. The myth of the impotent ruler, the waste land and the quest for a regenerative power appears in many forms in literature: for example, in *Oedipus Rex* by the Greek dramatist Sophocles (496–405BC); *Morte d'Arthur* by Sir Thomas Malory (1400–71), and *Idylls of the King* by Alfred, Lord Tennyson (1809–92). Wagner's operas, particularly *Parsifal* (1882), were also demonstrations to Eliot of how such myth material could be used in a modern artistic idiom.

From the manuscript of the poem, it appears that the title *The Waste Land* was a later thought. Large sections of what developed into the poem were grouped under the title, 'He Do the Police in Different Voices', a quotation from *Our Mutual Friend* (1864–5), the novel by Charles Dickens (1812–70), but, although it suited the scenes of social comedy in the early drafts, such a title would have been totally unsatisfactory for the poem that emerged. For Eliot the waste land is that area of human life where people exist without a guiding faith, where they have turned their backs on spiritual enlightenment, and the present title points to this dilemma.

EPIGRAPH (SHORT QUOTATION OR FRAGMENT USED TO PREFACE WORK)

'For I saw with my own eyes the Sibyl
of Cumae hanging in a cage and the boys were
talking to her: "What do you want, Sibyl?"
She answered, "I want to die"'.

The Sibyl was a Greek prophetess who, when consulted by people for her advice, gave enigmatic answers. She appealed to the God Apollo to grant her as many years of life as she had grains of sand in her hand. Her wish was granted; however, she neglected to ask Apollo to keep her young. She became older and older, more and more feeble, but she could not die. Life came to be an agony of boredom and, where she was placed in a basket in her shrivelled condition, she was tormented by groups of boys teasing her with their questions. The quotation comes from *The Satyricon* by Petronius, an author (first century AD) of the later Roman Empire who wrote about the vulgarity and decadence of the period. This story concerning the holy Sibyl is presented among other inconsequential incidents at a debauched banquet.

Eliot had intended to use as an epigraph the words 'The horror! The horror!' from the story *Heart of Darkness* (1902) by the Polish-born English novelist Joseph Conrad (1857–1924), but was dissuaded by Ezra Pound. Both the chosen and the discarded quotations suggest a vision of moral emptiness on the part of their original speakers; life has lost all its charm and death can only be a welcome release for the sufferer. The Sibyl is related to the other prophetic figures in the poem: Madame Sosostris, Tiresias, Old Testament prophetic voices, Buddha and the Voice of the Thunder.

THE DEDICATION

NOTES AND GLOSSARY

> **Ezra Pound** (1885–1972), American poet and close friend of Eliot (see note on the text)
>
> **il miglior fabbro** (*Italian*) 'the better craftsman'. Dante (*Purgatory* xxvi, 117) applauded the mastery of the Provençal poet, Arnaut Daniel, with these words. Eliot added the dedication to his poem in 1923 in gratitude to Ezra Pound for his help in shaping *The Waste Land* and in appreciation of Pound's skill as a poet

I THE BURIAL OF THE DEAD

The title of Part I, 'The Burial of the Dead', intimates the central concern of the whole poem as well as of Part I. What do we mean by 'life' and 'death'? Each religion, in its ceremonies concerning the dead, gives some particular answer to the question. Many of these religious answers rest on a belief in the possibility of resurrection or the contribution of the dead to the replenishing and perpetuation of life. In Christian terms, the sacrificial death of Jesus Christ, the God-man, is essential to the wellbeing of the world. In the non-Christian terms examined by James Frazer, the idea of sacrifice for the welfare of the tribe was extremely widespread.

Part I can be examined most easily by accepting Eliot's division of the seventy-six lines into four paragraphs or sections. Eliot's method requires that we move from section to section without looking for a kind of narrative continuity which he does not use; nor does he explain to us where he is going or what he is attempting to achieve. We must allow a pattern to emerge in our own minds.

In the first paragraph (lines 1–18), there are two units: lines 1–7 and lines 8–18. The two units overlap but, basically, the first is vegetal in emphasis and the second is social. The opening statement sounds paradoxical in that the month of April is traditionally seen in England as the first month of spring, gentle after the harshness of winter. Eliot seems to recall the opening lines of the General Prologue to *The Canterbury Tales* by Geoffrey Chaucer (1340–1400):

> Whan that Aprille with his shoures sote (sweet)
> The droghte of Marche hath perced to the rote ...
> Than longen folk to goon on pilgrimages.

Eliot's poem, too, is concerned with a kind of pilgrimage or quest but, at the start of his poem, the traditional signal does not prompt the inhabitants of the 'dead land' to thoughts of hope and departure, quite the reverse. Winter is seen as the comfortable season, maintaining as it had done a minimal life where action was not called for. The arrival of April is an agony to the speakers because it makes demands of them and reminds them of past and future ('memory and desire'). The lilacs of line 2 occur elsewhere in Eliot's work as suggesting powerful emotion and tenderness (see his poem 'Portrait of a Lady') and in the waste land emotion must be avoided. The main **imagery** of these lines is of vegetable life and the verbs in the present participle ('breeding', 'mixing', 'stirring', 'covering', 'feeding') emphasise a lack of motion.

The progression of the seasons continues in line 8 but the 'us' are now more human, existing in a world of parks and cafés. Among the smart people going round the fashionable places in Europe there is an anxiousness communicated in the abrupt shifts in the syntax of the speaker and in the restless movement from place to place. This is the Central Europe of the period around the First World War when the traditional aristocratic patterns and national boundaries were breaking up. The insistence by the Countess Marie that she is not Russian is possibly a reaction to the Communist Revolution in Russia in 1917 and a clinging to what she considers to be a more civilised nationality. The nervous, rootless mentality looks forward to the conversation of the rich woman in Part II.

Like the first paragraph, the second (lines 19–42) can be divided into two units. In the first of these units (lines 19–30), Eliot adopts a language strongly reminiscent of the prophetic books of the Old Testament. Just as the prophet Ezekiel was taken to the valley strewn with the bones of the dead and asked, 'Son of man, can these bones live?' so we are asked what life can come out of the wilderness of our world. Because we are spiritually dead we can envisage no possibilities but the unending routine of our journey through the desert of our days. What we must learn to understand is our condition of mortality, the fact of death and our present helplessness. The Cumaean Sibyl of the epigraph asked for unending life; she was granted her wish and her handful of dust became a rebuke to her.

The two questions from Wagner's opera provide a frame for the episode concerning the hyacinth girl. The story of Tristan and Isolde is one of the world's great love stories. The first quotation comes from the beginning of Wagner's opera on the subject; a sailor longs for his loved one. Later in the story the same words could be used by the wounded Tristan when he hopes for the arrival of Isolde from Ireland. His lookout on the sea cliffs tells him that there is no sign of her. His urgent hopes are disappointed and when she does eventually arrive the strain is too much for Tristan and he dies. In between the anticipation and disappointment of Tristan's love are set the anticipation and bewilderment of the lover of the hyacinth girl. The moment of intensity, of ecstasy, was built up to, but, at the very point when everything hoped for should have been realised, he had frozen and his vision had shown him what Tristan had experienced, the emptiness and futility of his love.

Throughout the poem various prophetic figures appear, including the Sibyl, Ezekiel, Tiresias, the Buddha, and the thunder of the final part. Madame Sosostris, with her bad cold, is an **ironic** version of the prophetic figure. Her name itself sounds like a cheap imitation of some Egyptian deity and the Tarot pack which, according to Jessie Weston, had played such a central part in the most crucial fertility rites of Ancient Egypt, has now become part of the equipment of a bogus fortune-teller. Nonetheless, the paradox of Madame Sosostris being 'the wisest woman in Europe, / With a wicked pack of cards', is continued in the fact that, however bogus she may appear to be or even try to be, her reading of the cards does foretell the events and characters of the poem. Little attempt is made by her to explain the cards and she offers only one piece of advice: 'Fear death by water' (drowning) but, in an indirect way, she indicates the nature of the waste land with its 'crowds of people, walking round in a ring', she sees the temptation of Belladonna and she points to the lack of spiritual enlightenment in the absence of the Hanged Man.

The description of London in the final paragraph of Part I provides evidence for Madame Sosostris's cryptic vision. Eliot, using a composite of Baudelaire's Paris, Dante's Hell and, according to Ezra Pound, the London of William Blake (1757–1827), creates a horrifying picture of people locked in a mindless, life-destroying routine. In Canto III of his *Hell*, Dante, after describing the stream of souls condemned for their spiritual emptiness, isolates one figure whom he recognises as a Pope who has been guilty of the cowardice of refusing high office and thereby allowing a wicked Pope to misgovern the Church. The figure of Stetson seems to be given a similar character by Eliot. By referring to Mylae, as well as to Dante's medieval Hell and Baudelaire's 'swarming city' of the nineteenth century, Eliot is anxious to stress that the problem he sees is not one unique to London in 1922, but is endemic to humankind. At one level, the conversation in the streets of London is a piece of macabre, surrealistic comedy, but, at its deeper level, the episode recalls the title of Part I, 'The Burial of the Dead' and the fertility rites which are so crucial to the meaning of the whole poem. Stetson, the reader, must tend the buried corpse, whether that corpse be an effigy of the god, a human sacrifice, or what the Bible calls 'the old man' which the Christian has to bury before a new life is possible (see Romans, Chapter 6). The Dog, a friend of human beings, could be any temptation to humans to look for easy solutions, short cuts or the kind of apathy or indolence described in the opening lines of the poem.

Notes and glossary

Title it comes from the burial service of the Anglican Church

7 **tubers** swollen roots providing nourishment for the future growth of a plant

8 **Starnbergersee** lake near Munich, in Bavaria, a fashionable resort visited by Eliot in 1911

9 **colonnade** a covered walk with columns, like an arcade

10 **Hofgarten** public park in Munich

12 **Bin gar ... deutsch** (*German*) 'I am not Russian at all, I come from Lithuania, pure German'

13 **the arch-duke's** the archduke Ferdinand of Austria was assassinated in 1914 and his death was one of the immediate causes of the First World War

15 **Marie** Countess Marie Larisch who had many family connections with the royal families of Austria and Bavaria. Her book, *My Past*, describing these connections appeared in 1913. Eliot had already met her

20 **Son of man** the phrase used by God to address his prophet Ezekiel in the Old Testament of the Bible (Ezekiel 2:1). Ezekiel is commanded to preach against the wickedness of the Israelites

22 **broken images** God tells Ezekiel that he will break the idols (images) erected by the Israelites to false gods

23 **the cricket no relief** the sound of the grasshopper gives no comfort in the desert

25–9 **There is ... meet you** these lines derive from the opening lines of Eliot's early poem, 'The Death of Saint Narcissus'

26 **red rock** in the Bible the prophet Isaiah predicts that, in a new, righteous kingdom, 'a man shall be as an hiding place from the wind, and a covert from the tempest; as rivers of water in a dry place, as the shadow of a great rock in a weary land.' (Isaiah 32:2)

30 **handful of dust** in biblical terms man's body comes from the dust and returns to dust

31–4 **Frisch ... du** (*German*) 'The wind blows fresh towards the homeland; my Irish child, where are you waiting?' The lines come from the beginning of Wagner's opera, *Tristan and Isolde*

35 **hyacinths** flowers symbolic of resurrection because, according to the Greek legend, they had sprung up from the blood of the slain youth Hyacinthus

42 ***Oed' ... das Meer*** (*German*) 'Waste and empty is the sea.' The line comes from the final Act of Wagner's *Tristan and Isolde*

43 **Madame Sosostris, famous clairvoyante** a fortune-teller whose name Eliot borrowed from a similar character in *Crome Yellow* (1921), a novel by Aldous Huxley (1894–1963). There was also a Madame Helena Blavatsky (1831–91) who was famous for her knowledge of magic

46 **pack of cards** Eliot does not mean the ordinary pack of playing cards but the Tarot pack, consisting of seventy-eight illustrated cards and widely used in casting horoscopes. Jessie Weston claimed that the cards dated back to ancient Egyptian times when they were used in the prediction of the rising and falling of the river Nile. She also connected the symbolism of the designs on the cards with the Grail story. In his note, Eliot concedes that he was not familiar with the exact details of the pack and there is little point in looking for the particular cards of the Tarot

47 **Phoenician Sailor** Phoenicia was the area on the Eastern Mediterranean coast now occupied by Lebanon and Syria. It was the location of the annual ceremonies to commemorate the death and resurrection of the god Thammuz, and was famous for its sailors and traders. See also comments on Part IV 'Death by Water'

48 **(Those are pearls that were his eyes.)** a line from Shakespeare's *The Tempest* (I.2.398). It comes from a song sung by Ariel suggesting to Ferdinand that his father, King Alonso, has been transformed by drowning into 'something rich and strange'. Compare line 126

49-50 **Belladonna ... of situations** in Italian, 'bella donna' means beautiful lady. Belladonna is also the name of a poisonous flower used in cosmetics. Eliot may be referring in these lines to a description by Walter Pater (1839–94) of the famous painting of Mona Lisa by Leonardo da Vinci (1452–1519): 'She is older than the rocks among which she sits; like the vampire, she has been dead many times, and learned the secrets of the grave; and has been a diver in deep seas, and keeps their fallen day about her; and trafficked for strange webs with Eastern merchants'

51 **man with three staves** in his note, Eliot says that this figure is associated by him, 'quite arbitrarily, with the Fisher King himself'. Although the poet claims that the man with the three staves is an 'authentic member of the Tarot pack', it is difficult to see which card he had in mind

51 **the Wheel** the cycle of Fortune

52 **one-eyed merchant** anticipates Mr Eugenides in line 209. He is 'one-eyed' because he appears in profile on the card and because he is a man of limited vision

53 **Which is blank ... see** according to Jessie Weston, the traders from the Levant acted as carriers for religious beliefs and legends such as the story of the Grail but they themselves did not necessarily understand the significance of their stories. Madame Sosostris has no comprehension of these mysteries

55 **Hanged Man** an actual figure in the Tarot pack. Eliot saw a connection between this figure and the Hanged God discussed by Frazer in *The Golden Bough* and he is associated by the poet with the hooded figure in line 363. The Hanged Man symbolises the sacrifice of one person or god to ensure the regeneration of fertility

57 **Thank you** she has been paid

Mrs Equitone a client of the fortune-teller

58 **horoscope** a plan of a person's character and prospects calculated by a study of the stars and planets prominent at the time of their birth

60 **Unreal City** the City in London is the business centre of London and the place where Eliot worked at the time of writing *The Waste Land*. In his note, Eliot refers to lines in Baudelaire's poem, 'The Seven Old Men': 'Swarming city, city full of dreams, where the ghost, in broad daylight, stops the passer-by'

61 **brown fog** the heavy fog mixed with the dirty smoke from factories

62 **London Bridge** bridge across the River Thames leading to the City

63 **I had not thought death had undone so many** Eliot takes the line from Dante's *Hell*, Canto III: 'such a long stream of people that I should never have believed that death had undone so many'. The people described had lived selfishly and had known neither good nor evil

64 **Sighs, short and infrequent, were exhaled** Eliot draws our attention to lines in Dante's *Hell*, Canto IV: 'Here, so far as I could tell, there was no lamentation except sighs, which caused the eternal air to tremble.' The sighs are uttered by those who had lived good lives but without Christian knowledge. In limbo, this part of Hell, the souls have desire for God but lack hope

66 **King William Street** in the City of London

67 **Saint Mary Woolnoth** a church in the City dating back to the twelfth century but restored and rebuilt in the seventeenth and eighteenth centuries. A report in 1920 suggested that it should be demolished; Eliot with others opposed this move

68 **dead sound on the final stroke of nine** the bell attached to the church clock does not strike properly on the ninth stroke. Nine a.m. is the hour when offices in the City would open for work. According to the Gospel, Christ died at the ninth hour and Eliot may have had this echo in his mind

69 **Stetson** Eliot claimed that he had no particular person in mind but wished to suggest the typical businessman of the City. The word 'stetson', however, is the name of the large hat worn by cowboys, and some people felt that Eliot must have been referring to Pound who wore such a hat. Eliot denied this

70 **Mylae** a battle (260BC) in the first Punic War between the Romans and the Carthaginians to determine who should control trade in the Mediterranean. The Carthaginians are related to the Phoenicians who appear elsewhere in the poem

71–5 **That corpse ... again!** According to a **myth** in Ancient Egypt, the semi-divine Osiris was murdered by his rival Set and the torn pieces of his body were buried in different places in Egypt. His wife, Isis, usually associated with the Nile, made those graves into holy places and each year grain was planted above them. When the grain sprouted, the people recognised that Osiris was not really dead but was resurrected in the new crops. An effigy of Osiris was also floated on the currents across the eastern Mediterranean from Alexandria to Byblos to symbolise the dying and rebirth of the year. Sirius, the Dog Star, was associated with the annual flooding of the Nile

74 **the Dog** Eliot refers us to *The White Devil*, V.4, by John Webster (1580–1638), where Cornelia is singing a lament for 'the friendless bodies of unburied men'. She goes on to say, 'But keep the wolf far hence, that's foe to men, / For with his nails he'll dig them up again.' Webster's 'wolf' is changed by Eliot to 'Dog' to fit the lines into the London street scene. The capital letter is Eliot's way of generalising the idea of the dog

76 **'You! hypocrite lecteur! – mon semblable, – mon frère'** (*French*) Eliot takes the line from the introductory poem, 'To the Reader,' in Baudelaire's *Flowers of Evil*. In the poem Baudelaire states that we are all guilty of 'stupidity, error, sin and meanness' but, worst of all, of boredom, spiritual emptiness, and he

involves the reader in his disgust by addressing him finally as, 'Hypocrite reader, my fellow man, my brother!'

II A GAME OF CHESS

In Thomas Middleton's *Women Beware Women* (1621), each move in the game of chess is matched by a move in the seduction of Bianca. It is a story of lust, manipulation and deceit. In this part of *The Waste Land*, Eliot, while focusing on two modern episodes, incorporates a wide range of references to women who were victims of lust and deceit.

The first episode (down to line 138) is given an elaborate, mock-epic setting. The description of the room carries memories of the meeting of famous lovers like Antony and Cleopatra and Dido and Aeneas but the ornateness of the decorations has an excessive and artificial quality. The convoluted syntax of the long sentences leads the reader into confusion but, as the description moves to the picture of Philomel, a more sinister element disturbs the mind. After Philomel was cruelly assaulted, she was given by the Gods the voice of the nightingale with which to proclaim the wrong done to her, but the world (and the 'hypocrite reader') still relentlessly pursues her. The sickly oppressiveness of the room leads into the claustrophobic hysteria of the woman.

The inverted commas indicate the words of the woman, anxious and questioning. The lines in between the woman's questions belong to her male companion and the lack of inverted commas suggests that we are overhearing his thoughts and not his words. He seems resigned and even playful, though in a macabre way, as if he has heard her frantic questions so often before that he knows proper replies to be useless. His state of mind, however, does not suggest health but a preoccupation with loss and death.

The second episode, beginning at line 139, is set in a pub in the Cockney area of London. Eliot, in a note on the typescript, said that he did not wish to indicate the Cockney pronunciation by using odd spelling but something of the intonation and style of Cockney English is communicated by him. The story told about Lil and Albert is sordid and lacking in any suggestion of love. Child-bearing is presented as a squalid burden, with the wife's health and appearance deteriorating and the husband unsympathetic and irresponsible. The characters are trapped in time and no human value is asserted to give them dignity. Eliot emphasises the pressure of time by his repetition of the barman's imperious call. The sad sweetness of Ophelia's farewell merges with the voices of those leaving the pub and acts partly as a contrast in its grave refinement and partly as a parallel in that Ophelia's story, like Lil's, is one of deceit and incomprehension.

Despite the obvious differences in setting, language and social class between the two episodes, they share certain qualities very central to Eliot's view of the waste land. Both present sterile relationships between men and women; in the first episode, the characters no longer even communicate: the woman voices nervous questions but the man remains silent and detached; in the second episode, Lil already looks 'antique' at the age of thirty-one and her main effort appears to be the prevention of further children. Behind the tawdry lives they live, where they seem like pawns in a game of chess rather than controllers, is the fear of decay and death, the cold 'wind under the door'.

Notes and glossary

The title a reference to the scene in the play *Women Beware Women* (1621) by Thomas Middleton (1580–1627), where Bianca is seduced by the Duke while her mother-in-law is diverted by a game of chess with the woman who has arranged the seduction. The original title, 'In the Cage', referred to the epigraph describing the fate of the Cumaean Sibyl

77 **The Chair ... throne** Eliot notes his debt to Shakespeare's *Antony and Cleopatra*, II.2 where Enobarbus describes Cleopatra's barge at her first meeting with Antony: 'The barge she sat in, like a burnished throne, / Burned on the water ...'. There are further echoes of Enobarbus's description in the following lines. 'Burnished' means polished

78 **glass** mirror

79 **standards wrought with fruited vines** columns decorated with moulded grapes and vine leaves

80 **Cupidon** a sculpted representation of the boy-god of love

82 **Doubled** (the mirror) reflected

candelabra elaborate candlesticks

86 **vials** small bottles

87 **synthetic** mixed, blended, but with a strong suggestion of artificiality

88 **Unguent** ointment

92 **laquearia** panelled ceiling. Eliot in his notes quotes from Book I of *Aeneid* by the Roman poet Virgil (70–19BC): 'flaming torches hang from the gold-panelled ceiling, and the torches conquer the night with flames'. The scene describes the banquet given by Dido, Queen of Carthage, in honour of Aeneas. He makes love to her but later deserts her

93 **coffered** panelled

94 **Huge sea-wood fed with copper** logs of driftwood (from the sea) with copper in them are burning in the fire. The salt and copper burn with orange and green flames

96 **dolphin** a symbol of love in medieval times

98 **sylvan scene** the wooded area around the Garden of Eden as seen by Satan intent on seducing man from God in John Milton's *Paradise Lost* (1667)

99 **The change of Philomel ... forced** Philomela (commonly known as Philomel) was raped by her brother-in-law, King Tereus, and he cut out her tongue to prevent her from telling her sister. The gods transformed her into a nightingale. The story is told in the *Metamorphoses* (changes of form), a Latin poem by Ovid (43BC–AD17)

101 **inviolable** cannot be injured or profaned

103 **'Jug Jug' to dirty ears** (a) the song of the nightingale (as represented in Elizabethan poetry); (b) 'jug' was also a form of vulgar sexual address. The same sound is heard differently by different listeners. See line 204

104 **withered stumps of time** old legends were depicted; also a reference to Philomel's ripped tongue

105 **staring forms** portraits, or figures in the paintings

115 **rats' alley** Eliot connects this line with line 195

126 **pearls** see note on page 16. Originally, Eliot's line read: 'The hyacinth garden. Those are pearls that were his eyes, yes!'

128 **0 0 0 0 that Shakespeherian Rag** a rag is a piece of jazz dance music. Eliot's line comes from 'The Shakespeherian Rag', a popular song of 1912 and has the **rhythm** typical of ragtime music

137 **game of chess** see note on title of this part. Originally, there was a line between the present lines 137 and 138 that read: 'The ivory men make company between us'

138 **lidless** sleepless, uncomfortable

139 **demobbed** short for 'demobilised', meaning released from the army back into civilian life

140 **I didn't mince my words** I told her directly

141 **HURRY UP PLEASE IT'S TIME** the call of the barman at closing time in a British pub (a shortened form of public house, a place where alcoholic drinks can be bought and consumed during certain hours fixed by law), telling people to finish their drinks and leave

152 **straight** challenging

153 **you can get on with it** you will have to accept it

158 **pulling a long face** adopting a dejected expression

159 **to bring it off** to induce an abortion

166 **gammon** smoked ham

170 **Ta ta** goodbye (*slang*)

171 **Good night ... good night** the line comes from Shakespeare's *Hamlet*, V.4. when Ophelia, driven mad by the death of her father and her confused love for Hamlet, bids farewell before going to drown herself

III THE FIRE SERMON

Just as in Part I, the title 'The Burial of the Dead' does not explain itself till Stetson's planted corpse appears at the end, so the force of the title 'The Fire Sermon' is not made clear till Eliot invokes the Buddha and St Augustine in the final lines of Part III. In his notes on these lines, Eliot stresses the importance he attaches to the teaching of those saints of east and west, both of whom had experienced the pleasures of the body before deciding to follow a spiritual path. In this part of the poem, Eliot presents a series of incidents that demonstrate his agreement with the decision of the two ascetic figures.

The first section (lines 173–86) uses Edmund Spenser's idealised vision of human love in the setting of an earthly paradise where the nymphs of the pure river celebrate the wedding as a background contrast to the example of casual, sordid modern sex. Nature itself is now spoiled and the clutching fingers of leaves suggest desperation. The recurring refrain from Spenser's joyful wedding poem now sounds plaintive or even mocking. What song can the poet sing in the brown land where the river is now polluted with the rubbish of uncaring people? This modern location is the land of captivity, of lamentation, and always the poet is made aware of how dead the land and the people have become.

Joining the second section (lines 187–202) to the first are echoes from the scene in James Joyce's *Ulysses* when Bloom goes to the funeral of Paddy Dignam: 'The rattle of bones', the rat, the canal and the gas-works all evoke the unpleasant episode of the funeral. In the gloomy industrial setting with its canal and gasworks the speaker, who is linked to Prince Ferdinand in *The Tempest*, fishes on a winter evening. The death of his father and brother who were both kings suggests that he is now king himself, the Fisher King of the wasteland. There seems little hope of his catching a fish in a polluted canal in winter and his thoughts are fixed on the unburied remains of his relatives. Spring has not yet arrived but it does not promise any purification or fertility. The hectic traffic of the city and the sordid relationship of Sweeney and Mrs Porter are in sad contrast to the heroic hunt and the encounter between the Goddess of chastity and Actaeon. Similarly, the farcical washing of the prostitutes' feet is a parody of the feet-washing ceremony in the chapel of the grail celebrated by the choir of boys.

The short section (lines 203–6) with the nightingale's song reminds us of the story of Philomel described in lines 99–103 and emphasises the themes of assaulted innocence and the power of lust.

In the following lines (207–14), Eliot reinforces his general claim that London, representative of urban living, is corrupt and has lost its spiritual vision. The Smyrna merchant, one-eyed we remember, is a decadent version of the Phoenician traders who, according to Jessie Weston, had transmitted knowledge of the fertility religions in the old days. The merchant's appearance, his unimpressive samples, his crude language, his suspect invitation, all indicate the fallen nature of the modern trader.

In 'The Fire Sermon' sexual relations are presented as violent or mechanical; respect and affection are absent. In the episode of the typist and the 'young man carbuncular', Eliot's concern is to show their mechanical behaviour. He opens the description by suggesting an automatic quality in the eyes and back of the office worker who is reduced in the monotony of his work to the status of a 'human engine'. The typist's life seems to be contained in the display of her clothes and food; she is bored and tired, has nothing to offer or withhold. The clerk accomplishes his sexual task without apparent pleasure and the actions do not affect either character. Do they have personalities that can be affected? The casual but obvious **rhymes** make each action predictable and dispassionate and nowhere is this more striking than in the final four lines (253–6) where the typist's easy acceptance of her dishonour is in contrast to the anguished song of Olivia in Goldsmith's novel *The Vicar of Wakefield* (1766).

The role of Tiresias in the poem is indicated in Eliot's note on line 218 and in this section he provides a crucial time dimension to the episode. In the particularities of his description and by involving contrasting examples from earlier periods (for example, Sappho and Goldsmith), Eliot seems to attribute a unique squalor to the modern world; Tiresias, however, assures us that he, with his comprehensive experience of the living and the dead, has seen all this before.

Line 257, 'This music crept by me upon the waters' refers back to the previous record on the gramophone, back also to Ferdinand in lines 191–2, and forward to 'The pleasant whining of a mandoline' (line 261). The line works differently with each of these references: the record with which the woman anaesthetises her feelings pervades the city and is a cold reminder of human insensitivity; the music Ferdinand heard was Ariel's song of consolation to him and this music might counteract the nastiness of the previous scene; the mandoline is a 'pleasant whining', a paradoxical description which combines pleasure and pain. This section (lines 257–65) certainly offers a pleasing sensation but there are hints that the sensation is flimsy and not to be trusted too far. The poet's, 'O City city,' has a distinctly solemn tone, the lounging fishmen are not fishermen and the glory of the church is a physical one and not necessarily spiritual.

For those readers who know Wagner's operas, it is easy to see a connection between the 'splendour of ... white and gold' (line 265) and the shining of the sacred gold in the river, the loss of which is lamented by the Rhine-maidens in the passage down to line 306. The opening description of the Thames is reminiscent of the description of the same river at the beginning of Joseph Conrad's *Heart of Darkness* (1902), a book greatly admired by Eliot, in which Conrad tries to show how precarious our civilisation is and how depraved the human heart can be. The modern and the renaissance Thames with its traffic has an obvious appeal but the lament of the Rhine-maidens reminds us that something has been lost. Even the spectacle of Queen Elizabeth in a golden barge like Cleopatra's, the sound of bells on the wind and the white towers cannot balance the lament. The three river-maidens tell the same story of violation and confusion; they appear to have no hope or impetus towards a new life. In the three accounts (lines 292–305) by the Thames-girls there is a progression in degradation as if the three reports could be by the same person describing her fall from honour, the situation 'After the event' and her descent into a state of madness where her world has fallen apart and even her command of language has broken down.

The final lines (307–11) of Part III do offer some hope in that the Buddha and St Augustine each came to an understanding of his problem and saw a way forward. St Augustine's expression of gratitude is the only explicit invocation of God in the entire poem. The spacing of these lines, however, with the final burning left trailing without a full stop, may suggest that there is no one final solution to the problem of human sin, or at least that it is not clear at this point in the poem.

NOTES AND GLOSSARY

The title in his note to line 308, Eliot refers his reader to the Buddha's Fire Sermon (fifth century BC). The Buddha tells his followers that the human senses, and all that they perceive, are burning: 'With what fire are they burning? I declare to you that they are burning with the fire of lust, with the fire of anger, with the fire of ignorance, with the concerns of birth, decay, death, grief, lamentation, misery, dejection and despair.' The follower who studies the scriptures and follows the Noble Path, becomes weary of the things of the senses and rids himself of all passion and so becomes free of the cycle of birth and death and rebirth. In Christianity, fire is a common symbol of lust and also of the purifying power of God

173 **river's tent** the leaves on the trees form an arch over the river

175 **nymphs** beautiful young girls in classical legend

176 **Sweet Thames, runs softly, till I end my song** the line comes from the refrain of *Prothalamion* by Edmund Spenser (1552–99). The poem celebrates an aristocratic wedding on the banks of the River Thames in beautiful surroundings in summer

179 **testimony** evidence

181 **addresses** addresses to which mail can be forwarded or at which the men can be found and made to fulfil their responsibilities to the girls

182 **waters of Leman** in the Bible, the Hebrews recall their exile in Babylon and how they longed for their homeland: 'By the rivers of Babylon, there we sat down, yea, we wept, when we remembered Zion ... How shall we sing the lord's song in a strange land?' (Psalm 137). Lake Leman is the French name for Lake Geneva in Switzerland near where Eliot received treatment for his mental illness in 1921 while he was writing part of *The Waste Land*. The archaic word 'leman' means a mistress

185 **But at my back ... to ear** Eliot's lines recall lines from 'To his Coy Mistress' by Andrew Marvell (1621–78): 'But at my back I always hear / Time's winged chariot hurrying near.' The poet urges the girl to make love with him because time and eventually death are pressing in on them

190 **gashouse** American word for gasworks

191 **Musing ... before him** Eliot refers the reader to Shakespeare's *The Tempest*: 'Sitting on a bank, / Weeping again the King my father's wreck, / This music crept by me upon the waters, / Allaying both their fury and my passion / With its sweet air' (I.2.389–92). Ferdinand is lamenting his father's death and is comforted by Ariel's music. See also lines 48 and 257

194 **garret** a small room in the attic

196 **But ... hear** see note above on 'But at my back ...'

196–8 **But ... in the spring** Eliot refers the reader to lines in *The Parliament of Bees*, a play by John Day (1574–1640): 'When of the sudden, listening, you shall hear, / A noise of horns and hunting, which shall bring / Actaeon to Diana in the spring, / Where all shall see her naked skin...' Actaeon was out hunting, according to the Greek legend, when he came on Diana, the goddess of chastity, bathing with her nymphs. As a punishment for his lack of self-control he was changed into a stag and hunted to death by his own hounds. Sweeney is a character who represents brutish vigour and sexual vulgarity. Mrs Porter is a woman of doubtful virtue (see following note)

199 **O the moon ... water** Eliot took these lines from a polite version of a vulgar ballad popular among Australian soldiers in the First World War. Mrs Porter may have been a famous brothel-keeper. The moon was special to the goddess Diana and a symbol of her purity. The 'soda water' is a cleaning solution not a drink

202 ***Et, O ces voix d'enfants, chantant dans la coupole!*** (*French*) 'And, O those children's voices singing in the dome!' The line comes from 'Parsifal' by

Paul Verlaine (1844–96). The poem, following Wagner's opera, describes
how the questing hero Parsifal has withstood all temptations and succeeded
in curing the wounded king, Amfortas (the Fisher King). Parsifal's feet are
washed and the choir of boys in the chapel of the Holy Grail sing a song of
celebration. The ceremony of feet-washing derives from the episode in the
Bible (John 13) where Jesus washes the feet of his disciples in an act of
humility and purification

203-6 **Twit ... Tereu** the song of the raped Philomel transformed into a nightingale
harks back to lines 99–103. Eliot also borrows from a song by John Lyly
(1554–1606): 'What bird so sings, yet so does wail? / Oh, 'tis the ravished
nightingale, / Jug, jug, jug, jug, tereu, she cries, / And still her woes at
midnight rise.' 'Twit' is a common imitation of bird song; 'tereu' means
'O, Tereus' (the king who raped Philomel)

209 **Mr Eugenides, the Smyrna merchant** Smyrna is the old name for Izmir, a
seaport in western Turkey, and it can be connected with Phoenician places
and people elsewhere in the poem. The name 'Mr Eugenides' means
'well-born' but, like 'Mrs Equitone' (line 57), it sounds artificial. Eliot, in
his notes, connects this merchant with 'the one-eyed merchant' (line 52)
and with the Phoenician Sailor (line 47) who appears as Phlebas in Part IV

211 **C.i.f. London: documents at sight** Eliot explains that the price of the
merchant's currants includes 'cost, insurance and freight to London' and
that the ownership papers for the currants would be given to the buyer in
London on receipt of a bank draft

212 **demotic** vulgar, uneducated

213 **Cannon Street Hotel** a hotel beside a railway station in the City of London.
This station served the routes to Continental Europe and the hotel was,
consequently, popular with travelling businessmen

214 **the Metropole** fashionable hotel in Brighton, on the south coast of England,
about one hour's journey from London. A 'weekend in Brighton' can suggest
an illicit sexual meeting

215 **violet hour** dusk when the sky can be a purplish-blue colour. The flower, the
violet, was, perhaps because of its use in perfumes, associated through
classical and medieval times with sex

216 **human engine** worker

218 **I Tiresias ... can see** Eliot's note reads: 'Tiresias, although a mere spectator
and not indeed a "character", is yet the most important personage in the
poem, uniting all the rest. Just as the one-eyed merchant, seller of currants,

melts into the Phoenician Sailor, and the latter is not wholly distinct from Ferdinand Prince of Naples, so all the women are one woman, and the two sexes meet in Tiresias. What Tiresias *sees*, in fact, is the substance of the poem.'

He then quotes the story of Tiresias from *Metamorphoses* by Ovid: 'Jupiter jokingly said to Juno, "You women receive much more pleasure in love than men do." Juno denied the claim. They decided to ask the wise Tiresias for his opinion because he knew love from both sides. Once, when two huge snakes were copulating in the green forest, he had struck them with his stick; he was miraculously transformed into a woman and lived as a female for seven years. In the eighth year he again saw the snakes and said: "If a blow of my stick had the magic to change my sex, I shall now strike you again." He struck the snakes, and he was restored to his original sex. For this reason he was asked to judge the Gods' playful argument; he supported Jupiter. Juno, it is claimed, was needlessly angered and she condemned the judge, Tiresias, to everlasting blindness. It is not permitted for one god to reverse the act of another god, but the all powerful father, to recompense Tiresias for the loss of his sight, gave him the power to know the future and so honoured Tiresias.'

Tiresias was the most famous prophet of the classical world

220–1 **At the ... sea** Eliot had in mind the coastal fishermen who return to port at dusk. He refers us to lines by Sappho, the sixth century BC Greek poetess: 'Thou, evening star, who draws homeward all that the radiant dawn sent out ...' There is an echo of the end of 'Requiem' by R.L. Stevenson (1850–94): 'Home is the sailor, home from sea, / And the hunter home from the hill'

225 **combinations** undergarments

227 **camisoles, and stays** undergarments and corsets (artificial support for her figure)

228 **old man with wrinkled dugs** Tiresias has shrivelled female breasts as part of his bisexuality (see note above on 'I Tiresias ...')

231 **carbuncular** with pimples or boils

233–4 **One ... millionaire** Bradford is a town in the north of England that manufactures woollen goods. Many manufacturers made large profits during the First World War and the lines suggest the vulgarity of newly acquired wealth. The north of England is often considered vulgar and unsophisticated by cultured Londoners and Eliot is sharing that prejudice

235 **propitious** suitable, favourable

243 **foresuffered** experienced; one who has felt pain before

245 **I who ... wall** in *King Oedipus* by Sophocles (495–406BC) the prophet
Tiresias knows that the city of Thebes is suffering sterility and plague
because Oedipus has unknowingly killed his father and married his own
mother and the gods have cursed the city

246 **And walked ... dead** in *The Odyssey* by Homer (about eighth century BC)
when Odysseus visits Hades (the Greek underworld of the dead), he is
advised by Tiresias who, though dead, still sees the future of the living

247 **patronising** as if he thinks he is doing her an honour

253-6 **When ... the gramophone** Eliot refers his reader to the novel, *The Vicar of
Wakefield* by Oliver Goldsmith (1730–74). Olivia who has been seduced
sings: 'When lovely woman stoops to folly, / And finds too late that men
betray, / What charm can soothe her melancholy? / What art can wash
her guilt away? / The only art her guilt to cover, / To hide her shame from
every eye, / To give repentence to her lover, / And wring his bosom,
is – to die'

257 **'This music ... waters'** see note on page 26 on 'Musing ... before him'

258 **the Strand** one of the main streets in London, joining Westminster to the
City. Formerly, its big houses backed onto the River Thames
Queen Victoria Street in the City and close to the Thames

259 **O City city** possibly an **allusion** to the cry of Jesus against the blindness of
the city of Jerusalem of his time: 'O Jerusalem, Jerusalem, thou that killest
the prophets, and stonest them that are sent unto thee, how often would I
have gathered thy children together, even as a hen gathereth her chickens
under her wings, and ye would not! Behold, your house is left unto you
desolate' (Matthew 23)

260 **Lower Thames Street** in the City on the Thames

261 **mandoline** a stringed musical instrument

263 **fishmen** workers from the nearby Billingsgate fishmarket

264 **Magnus Martyr** the church of St Magnus Martyr, near London Bridge and
the fishmarket, was rebuilt in the seventeenth century after the Great Fire of
London had destroyed it. Its interior was designed by the architect Sir
Christopher Wren (1632–1723). Eliot campaigned for its restoration

265 **Inexplicable** cannot be explained
Ionian one of the three styles of Grecian architecture. In the original
manuscript Eliot described the style as 'Corinthian'. Although these names

have a strictly technical sense, it is possibly significant that both 'Ionian' and 'Corinthian' can be used to mean decadent

266– **The river ... la la** Eliot points out that 'the Song of the (three) Thames-
306 daughters begins here. From line 292 to 306 inclusive they speak in turn.' He compares his Thames-daughters with the Rhine-maidens in Wagner's opera, *The Twilight of the Gods*. The Rhine-maidens lament the sacred gold that has been stolen from the River Rhine and the theft has brought a dullness to the river. At the end of the story the gold in the shape of a ring is recovered by the maidens from a huge fire in which the bodies of the hero and heroine have been burned

266 **sweats** the oil and tar in the river come to the surface and float like sweat on skin

273 **wash** the wave caused by the boat's movement

275 **Greenwich reach** stretch of the Thames downstream from the centre of London

276 **Isle of Dogs** the bank of the river opposite Greenwich, part of London's dock area

277 **Weialala ... leialala** the chorus from the Rhine-maidens' lament (see note on 'The river ...'above)

279 **Elizabeth and Leicester** Queen Elizabeth I of England and Lord Robert Dudley, the Earl of Leicester, one of the Queen's favourites. Eliot refers the reader to a letter written in 1561 by the Spanish Ambassador to his master King Philip of Spain in which he describes Elizabeth and Leicester: 'In the afternoon we were in a barge, watching the games on the river. She was alone with the Lord Robert and myself on the poop, when they began to talk nonsense and went so far that Lord Robert at last said, as I was on the spot [he was a bishop] there was no reason why they should not be married if the Queen pleased.' Elizabeth never got married, had no children and was proud of her title, the Virgin Queen

293 **Highbury ... Undid me** Eliot imitates words from Dante's *Purgatory*: 'Remember me, who am La Pia (Piety); Siena made me, Maremma undid me.' Siena and Maremma are places in Tuscany in Italy and La Pia was murdered by her husband. She is in Purgatory because she died before she had repented her life. Highbury is a residential area of London; Richmond and Kew are popular places to go to on boating trips

295 **Supine** lying on her back

296 **Moorgate** poorer area in the City

300 **Margate Sands** a seaside resort on the Thames estuary, popular for day-trips
from London. Eliot began *The Waste Land* in Margate when he was ill in
October 1921

306 **la la** the fading echo of the Rhine-maidens' lament

307 **To Carthage then I came** Eliot takes the line from the *Confessions* of St
Augustine (354–430): 'To Carthage then I came, where a cauldron of
unholy loves sang all about my ears.' St Augustine, born in what is now
Algeria, went to Carthage when he was sixteen and experienced the power of
lust before he gradually discovered the value of spiritual love

308 **Burning burning burning burning** see note on the title, 'The Fire Sermon'

309 **O Lord ... out** Eliot refers the reader to St Augustine's *Confessions*: 'I
entangle my steps with these outward beauties, but Thou pluckest me out,
O Lord, Thou pluckest me out.' In the Bible (Zechariah 3:2), God rescues
the corrupt high-priest from his sin and asks Satan, 'Is this not a brand
plucked out of the fire?' Eliot comments that, 'The collocation of these two
representatives (Buddha and St Augustine) of eastern and western
asceticism, as the culmination of this part of the poem, is not an accident.'

IV DEATH BY WATER

The original manuscript of Part IV had ninety-three lines and the deleted
sections do help us to a fuller understanding of the surviving ten lines.
A dead sailor, resembling Coleridge's Ancient Mariner, recounts the
story of a fishing trip which ended in disaster. The story has close links
with the final voyage of the Greek hero Odysseus (Ulysses) imagined by
Dante (*Hell*, xxvi) and Tennyson. Ulysses was seen by Dante and
Tennyson as a man with an insatiable curiosity, unable to accept the idea
of his dying, and driven to seek new experiences. His attitude is the
extreme opposite of that of the Buddha and St Augustine expressed at the
end of Part III. Furthermore, the surviving lines about Phlebas are
virtually a translation of the final part of Eliot's poem, 'In the Restaurant',
written in French some four years earlier. In that poem a dirty old waiter
tells a customer how, at the age of seven, he had been on the point of
having sex with a young girl when he was interrupted by the arrival of a
big dog and he ran away. The following lines about Phlebas come after
the waiter's sordid story: 'Phlebas the Phoenician, a fortnight drowned,

forgot the cries of gulls and the swell of the Cornish seas and the profit and the loss, and the cargo of tin. An undersea current carried him very far, taking him back through the stages of his former life. Just imagine, it was a hard fate, considering he was once a tall, handsome man.' The implication is that Phlebas, like the waiter, had sought physical pleasure and not spiritual wisdom.

The waiter's story also helps to connect Phlebas with Mr Eugenides more securely. St Paul, who was specially concerned with preaching the gospel to the Gentiles, wrote to his fellow missionary, Timothy: 'But they that will be rich fall into temptation and a snare, and into many foolish and hurtful lusts, which drown men in destruction and perdition' (1 Timothy 6:9). The merchant is trapped in his ambitions. Eliot, so fascinated by Conrad's account of Kurtz's degeneration in *The Heart of Darkness* (1902), must have remembered the story-teller's question:

> Did he live his life again in every detail of desire, temptation, and surrender during that supreme moment of complete knowledge? He cried in a whisper at some image, at some vision – he cried out twice, a cry that was no more than a breath – 'The horror! The horror!'

Phlebas has passed beyond such urgency but, in entering the whirlpool, he is locked in the cycle of his futile life, his death is fruitless. Jessie Weston, in her book, discusses how a wooden effigy of the god of fertility was thrown into the sea at Alexandria and carried by the current to the Phoenician coast, a symbol of the dying and rebirth of the year, a fruitful death by water. Eliot warns the reader to learn from the sad example of Phlebas and give careful thought to the direction of his life.

NOTES AND GLOSSARY

> **The title** an apparent contrast to 'The Fire Sermon' and burning of Part III. Compare also lines 47 and 55
>
> 312 **Phlebas the Phoenician** according to Eliot's note on line 218 he is a further aspect of the one-eyed merchant Mr Eugenides
>
> 315 **current** the flow of water may be a mocking pun on his pocket full of dried grapes (compare line 210)

319 **Gentile or Jew** a Gentile is any non-Jewish person. In the New Testament the two are taken to include all mankind and both are equally welcome to the gift of Christianity

320 **wheel** steering wheel of a boat; also the wheel of fortune (compare line 51)
windward the direction from which the wind is blowing

V WHAT THE THUNDER SAID

The first fifty lines of Part V are set in the bleak desert landscape visited briefly in Part I and the longed for rain is not seen to arrive throughout Part V. There is an atmosphere of remembered drama lapsing into anticlimax in lines 322–30. After the momentous and painful last hours of Jesus's life, the man whom his followers had believed was a god is dead. In lines reminiscent of the words of the inhabitants of the dead land (lines 1–7), they accept a minimal life without obvious hope of a resurrection; only the distant rolling of thunder beyond the mountains suggests spring and a new start.

In the second paragraph (lines 331–58), Eliot describes the journey through the waste land. The questing knight in his search for the Grail has to travel through inhospitable territory where he is subject to horrifying delusions. Hope on this journey in the desert is merely hypothetical: the form of the paragraph is determined by a series of 'ifs' with their answering 'buts'. The desert takes on a malevolent appearance, taunting and frightening the traveller. Water, the source of life, is totally absent. In the first paragraph the controlling word is 'after'; now, after the death of the god, the wounding of the Fisher King, the loss of personal faith, man must confront his own impotence.

Paragraphs three and four (lines 359–76) can be taken together. Eliot indicates in his notes that he is describing the journey to Emmaus and the decay of Eastern Europe manifested in the Communist Revolution in Russia. The disciples of Jesus, stunned by his death, are so blinded by their own helplessness that when the resurrected Jesus appears they fail to recognise him. Reality and hallucination cannot be distinguished by them. In his final message to his followers, Jesus warned of cruel times to come when there would be oppression and false prophets. For Eliot, Russian Communism with its atheist creed offers deluding prophecies to the blinded masses, and now they stumble about in their spiritual desert. Russia, however, is not unique but merely one aspect of the cycle of error and destruction seen throughout history. All men share the tendency to accept the unreal world as if it were the real. Eliot here suggests the contrast, specifically described by St Augustine, between the City of Destruction with its false values and the City of God with its Christian values.

Both the journey to Emmaus and the swarming over plains are examples of misguided pilgrimages but enlightenment can take place in unlikely circumstances. These two journeys are aspects of the knight's journey in search of the Grail. In the following two paragraphs (lines 377–94) the horrifying details of the knight's journey are described. Many of these details remind us of times which have occurred earlier in the poem; just as the five questions in lines 359–71 echo the anxious questions of the woman in Part II, her room is recalled and turned upside down in lines 377–81. The knight's ordinary power of perception is upset and he is mocked by echoes and hallucinations. His mind is on the edge of madness and the ruined chapel in its desolate location in the deceptive moonlight seems like a cruel joke after the agonies of his journey. The omens are not promising but the appearance of the cock heralds a new dawn and the flash of lightning intimates the arrival of the long awaited rain. In the knight's acceptance of his own emptiness, a miracle can take place.

The thunder section (lines 395–422) seems to occur parallel to the climax of the quest for the Holy Grail and even takes the place of the expected questions to the Grail. The country of India is still in the dry season and nature awaits the coming of the rain. In this case, however, the thunder announces not rain but the advice by which men's lives can be revitalised. As at the end of Part III where St Augustine and the Buddha are united, Eliot is intent here on joining western and eastern wisdoms together. Eliot may also be making a criticism of the state of the Christian church in Europe and suggesting that westerners have to look outside their over-familiar systems to find fresh inspiration in the east; this reading of Eliot's intention squares with the gloomy thought in lines 410–16. Eliot chooses to go back to an older wisdom whose very language lies behind all the varied developments of the Indo-European peoples. The words of advice (give, sympathise, control) heard in the sound of the thunder are straightforward and are central to the major religions. In the waste land, these virtues are absent.

Eliot presents three confessions illustrating the mentality of the waste land in an attempt to diagnose the spiritual emptiness that results from ignoring the teaching of the thunder. In the first, it is difficult to determine to whom it is addressed; 'my friend' was originally 'my brother' and it seems likely that the reader is being confided in. It is possible also that, if the surrender is sexual, the 'I' could be female and, indeed, the encounter described has a similarity to Francesca's account to Dante of her fateful love for Paulo (*Hell*, V). This account, however, has little in common with the various surrenders in Part III, 'The Fire Sermon': the speaker here is trembling with emotion and the surrender is a supreme moment, a moment of giving. There is, nonetheless, an undoubted suggestion of folly which 'an age of prudence can never retract'. Such is the general dullness of the person's life that this moment is unique but secret and it does not appear in the public or official accounts of his life. Mention of empty rooms, obituaries and the solicitor suggests that he considers himself already dead but there are parallels between this experience and the relationship with the hyacinth girl in Part I.

In answer to the challenge to sympathise or show compassion, the speaker confesses that, from his point of view, each individual is separated from all others and such is the self-centredness of people that they live locked away from each other. Both Count Ugolino and Coriolanus were led by their self-seeking nature into treachery against their own people and, because they can show no sympathy for others, they bring on themselves cruel punishment. The woman in the room in 'A Game of Chess' is similarly imprisoned in her own anxious mentality.

The third aspect of giving, according to the thunder, is control and, in particular, self-restraint. The connection between giving and control is not immediately obvious but Eliot's example does help to explain the connection. Without self-control one cannot give to another. If Coriolanus, for example, had learned to restrain his arrogance he could have communicated with his fellow Romans but he was so concerned with his image of himself, 'the key', that he could not appreciate the situation around him. Eliot uses the analogy of sailing to explore what can take place between two people. The good sailor does not impose rigid control on his boat; he accepts the power of wind and water and bases his steering of the boat on his understanding of this power. The boat 'responded gaily' as if glad to cooperate with man and wind and sea. Unfortunately, there are few other examples of this cooperative activity between man and nature elsewhere in the poem. Too often, as in both the episodes in Part II, the opposite happens and people choose to live artificially. The speaker in line 420 says, 'your heart would have responded' as the boat had but this verb is conditional and he cannot offer the right control, the appropriate invitation. He cannot do so because he has no self-control. Lines 279–89 offer a comparable situation where Elizabeth and Leicester have the chance to develop a relationship of mutuality but, instead, they turn the situation into a silly game and so remain trapped in their own solitudes.

The three virtues advocated by the thunder are not to be separated from each other; they depend on each other and, in a sense, are interchangeable. They are reasserted in the second last line of the poem, but before that line Eliot introduces some difficult fragments. The Fisher King, the quester, has crossed the waste land and reached the open sea. The chapel has been reached and the thunder has told how health can be restored to the people. In his question: 'Shall I at least set my lands in order?' there is a movement towards some positive action but there also appears to be a concession on his part that whatever he can do is very limited. The quotations that follow (lines 426–9) do not resolve our difficulty in understanding what he means. The line from the nursery rhyme and the line from de Nerval's poem 'The Disinherited' suggest that he is surrounded by ruins; the lines from Dante and *The Vigil of Venus* look forward to the possibility of new life. As if he sees the reader's difficulty, the king tells us that he has to take comfort where he can find it and it is fragmentary. His appeal to the swallow in line 428 is equally ambivalent. The reader by now knows the tragic story of Philomel and Procne and how they continue, as birds, to lament their fate. The swallow of Tennyson's poem carries a message of love and traditionally in England the swallows flying from the south announce the coming of summer; the bird is a good omen and, according to a legend, it flew over the crucified Jesus singing, 'Console'.

This apparent confusion is probably deliberate. Throughout the poem, Eliot has used many techniques to widen the scope and application of his vision of life. At the end of each part, the reader feels himself or herself addressed and the 'hypocrite reader' is caught again at the end of the poem. Hieronymo, driven partly mad by the cruelty and deceit around him, turns on the reader who thinks that the Fisher King is the man with the problem. Eliot forces the problems of the waste land on us because we, whether we know it or not, are the citizens of the 'unreal city' and we must find our Grail. The thunder repeats its advice and the mocking voice of Hieronymo is softened by the benediction of the last line.

NOTES AND GLOSSARY

> **The title** in the Bible, God is often described as speaking to men with a voice of thunder. Thunder commonly intimates the arrival of rain. Eliot refers specifically to the message of the thunder given in Brihadaranyaka-Upanishad, one of the books in Sanskrit sacred to Hinduism (see note on page 39: 'Then spoke …')
>
> 322 **torchlight … faces** a band of men came at night to arrest Jesus when he was betrayed by Judas
>
> 323–4 **frosty … places** in the garden called Gethsemane, Jesus prayed but his disciples could not keep awake. In St Luke's account, Jesus, 'Being in an agony … prayed more earnestly: and his sweat was as it were great drops of blood falling down to the ground'
>
> 326 **Prison and palace** the arrest of Jesus and his preliminary trial in the palace of the High Priest of the Jews before he was taken before Pilate, the Roman Governor in Jerusalem
>
> 326–7 **reverberation / Of thunder** according to the account in the Bible, at the death of Jesus the earth shook and a sudden darkness took place. As well as the re-echoing of the thunder, Eliot may have used 'reverberation' in its older sense of painful beating to refer to the beating inflicted on Jesus
>
> 339 **carious** decayed, rotten
>
> 346 **If there were water** (this does not count as a separate line but is numbered with 'And no rock')
>
> 353 **cicada** grasshopper characterised by its dry chirping noise (compare line 23) and related to the locust which eats all green growth and makes cultivated land into a desert
>
> 356 **hermit-thrush … drop** a shy North American bird celebrated, according to Eliot, for its 'water-dripping song'. The reference to the hermit-thrush and the following lines are reminiscent of 'When Lilacs Last in the Dooryard

Bloom'd', the **elegy** written for President Abraham Lincoln in 1865 by Walt Whitman.

359–65 **Who ... side of you?** Eliot refers the reader to the account of his expedition in the Antarctic by Sir Ernest Shackleton (1874–1922) in which he describes how 'the party of explorers, at the extremity of their strength, had the constant delusion that there was one more member than could actually be counted.' Eliot also had in mind the account by St Luke of two disciples journeying on the road from Jerusalem to Emmaus after the death of their master, Jesus: 'And it came to pass, that, while they communed together and reasoned, Jesus himself drew near, and went with them. But their eyes were holden that they should not know him' (Luke 24:15–16)

366–76 **What is that sound ... unreal** in his note, Eliot quotes a passage from *Glimpse into Chaos* (1920) by Herman Hesse (1877–1962): 'Already half of Europe, already at least half of Eastern Europe, on the way to chaos, drives drunkenly in spiritual frenzy along the edge of the abyss, and sings drunkenly, as though singing hymns, as Dmitri Karamazov [in *The Brothers Karamazov* by Fyodor Dostoevsky (1821–81)] sang. The offended bourgeois laughs at the songs; the saint and the seer hear them with tears.' Hesse was writing particularly about the Russian Revolution of 1917

367 **Murmur of maternal lamentation** Eliot may be referring to St Luke's account of the crucifying of Jesus in which he writes: 'And there followed him a great company of people, and of women, which also bewailed and lamented him. But Jesus turning into them said, "Daughters of Jerusalem, weep not for me, but weep for yourselves, and for your children"' (Luke 23:27–8)

368 **hooded** blindfolded

372 **reforms** takes a new shape

374 **Jerusalem ... London** centres of civilisations

378 **fiddled** played as if on a violin

383 **reminiscent** prompting memories

383–4 **bats ... wells** the movement of Surrealism, fashionable in 1922, presented ordinary things in an extraordinary way so as to show them as comic or horrific. Eliot acknowledged a debt to Hieronymus Bosch (1460–1516), one of the models for the Surrealists of the twentieth century and whose paintings of Hell have details similar to those in Eliot's lines. In medieval versions of the quest for the Grail, the quester has to pass through temptations and horrors to prove his courage and faith

384 **empty ... wells** in the Bible God tells his prophet Jeremiah: 'My people have committed two evils; they have forsaken me, the fountain of living waters, and carved themselves out cisterns, broken cisterns that can hold no water' (Jeremiah 2:13)

387 **tumbled ... empty chapel** there is nothing in the Perilous Chapel and Perilous Cemetery to offer promise or hope to the quester. His last temptation is despair

391 **cock** the cockerel announces the coming of daybreak and so, traditionally, it banishes ghosts and the powers of darkness. In Christian terms the cock crowing is firmly associated with Peter's denial of Jesus at the time of his trial in the palace of the High Priest. In his original manuscript Eliot has a 'black cock', commonly sacrificed in rituals to remove bad spirits

    rooftree the main beam supporting the ridge of the roof of the ruined chapel

395 **Ganga** Ganges, the sacred river of India

397 **Himavant** holy mountain in the Himalayas between India and Tibet

399– **Then spoke ... DA** Eliot takes the story of the thunder from the
400 Brihadaranyaka-Upanishad, one of India's holy books. Prajapati, the Creator, has three groups of offspring: gods, men and demons; they each seek his wisdom. To each he utters the syllable, 'DA', and asks if they understand. The gods think that he says, 'Restrain yourselves (damyata)', and he agrees. The men think that he says, 'Give (datta)', and he agrees. The demons think that he says 'Be compassionate (dayadhvam)', and he agrees. 'This same thing does the divine voice, thunder, repeat: "DA! DA! DA!" that is, restrain yourselves, give, be compassionate.' 'DA' is the Sanskrit root of words relating to 'give'; it is also an imitation of the sound of thunder

401 ***Datta*** give

404 **age** old age or later years of life

    retract withdraw, wipe out

406 **obituaries** brief biographies of the recently dead

407 **memories ... spider** Eliot refers the reader to lines from *The White Devil* (1612) by John Webster: 'O men / That lie upon their death-beds, and are haunted / With howling wives, ne'er trust them, they'll remarry / Ere the worm pierce your winding-sheet: ere the spider / Make a thin curtain for your epitaphs'. The characters in the play are strikingly passionate and deceitful. 'Beneficent' means kind or generous

408 **under seals** locked away and not to be opened before the person's death

411 ***Dayadhvam*** be compassionate, sympathise

411–12 **I have ... only** Eliot refers to the story of Count Ugolino related in Dante's *Hell* (xxxiii). Ugolino, because of his political treachery, was locked up with his four sons in a tower and eventually they all died of hunger, the father being the last to die. He says, 'I heard below the door of the horrible tower nailed up ... I did not weep, I so turned to stone inside.' In Hell he is dedicated to utter hatred against the man who had locked him in his prison

413 **We think ... the key** in his note Eliot quotes from F.H. Bradley's *Appearance and Reality* (1893): 'My external sensations are no less private to my self than are my thoughts or my feelings. In either case my experience falls within my own circle, a circle closed on the outside; and, with all its elements alike, every sphere is opaque to the others which surround it ... In brief, regarded as an existence which appears in a soul, the whole world for each is peculiar and private to that soul'

415 **aethereal rumours** vague, overheard comments by others or, more probably, his own insubstantial dreams

416 **broken Coriolanus** central character in Shakespeare's *Coriolanus*, he was brought up to despise the feelings of other people. His overwhelming pride and arrogance forced him into exile to fight with his previous enemies against his native Rome. The desperate appeal of his mother finally broke his self-confidence

418 *Damyata* control

423–4 **I ... Fishing** the Fisher King has crossed his waste land and arrived at the sea

424 **arid** the land is still barren

425 **Shall ... order?** in the Book of Isaiah, the land of Israel is described as made waste by the Assyrian invaders and 'In those days was King Hezekiah sick unto death. And Isaiah the prophet ... came unto him, and said unto him, "Thus saith the Lord, Set thine house in order; for thou shalt die, and not live"' (Isaiah 38:1). Hezekiah prays for mercy and is granted fifteen extra years of life and the promise that the land will prosper

426 **London Bridge ... down** the line comes from a children's rhyme which probably had its origin in the ritual of human sacrifice in blessing new buildings

427 *Poi ... affina* Eliot takes the line from a passage in Dante's *Purgatory* (xxvi) where the Provençal poet Arnaut Daniel, condemned to burn for his lust during life, asks for Dante's sympathy: '"And so I pray you, by that virtue which guides you to the top of the stair, remember later on my pain." Then

he hid himself in the fire which refines them.' Elsewhere Eliot speaks of the hope given by chosen suffering

428 **Quando ... chelidon** 'When shall I be like the swallow?' The line comes from an anonymous Late Latin poem, *The Vigil of Venus*, which celebrates the arrival of spring and Venus, the goddess of love. The poem concludes with a passage about the raped Philomel (see note to line 99) who, in this account, was transformed into a swallow and her sister, Procne, into a nightingale. She asks when the spring will come for her, when she will become like the swallow and be able to sing. The refrain of the poem promises love to all

428 **O swallow swallow** Eliot could be referring to a simple love song in 'The Princess' by Tennyson beginning, 'O swallow, swallow,' or to the poem 'Itylus' (Philomel) by Algernon Swinburne (1837–1909) beginning, 'Swallow, my sister, O sister swallow, / How can thine heart be full of the spring?'

429 *Le Prince ... abolie* (*French*) 'The Prince of Aquitaine in the ruined tower.' The line comes from the poem 'The Disinherited' by Gerard de Nerval (1808–55); de Nerval suffered from fits of madness and felt an acute loneliness. One of the cards in the Tarot pack shows a tower struck by lightning and a Dark Tower occurs in some of the Grail stories

430 **These fragments ... ruins** the 'fragments' may describe the bits of quotations in the previous few lines or the whole of Eliot's poem. 'Shored' means piled up as a support and the 'ruins' could refer to the 'ruined tower' of the previous line or, in a more general way, to the chaos and waste he sees around him. 'Shore' can also mean to land from the sea and the Fisher King may be describing his catch

431 **Why then ... againe** 'Hieronymo's mad again' is the subtitle of *The Spanish Tragedy* (1594), a play by Thomas Kyd (1557–95). Hieronymo's son has been murdered and, unknown to the murderers, Hieronymo knows exactly what has happened. When asked by the murderers if he can help to entertain their fathers with a show, Hieronymo replies: 'Why then, Ile fit you. Say no more. / When I was young, I gave my mind / And plied myself to fruitless poetry, / Which though it profit the professor naught / Yet is it passing pleasing to the world.'
Hieronymo sees his chance to gain his revenge and devises a play in which the parts, in different languages, are played by the people involved in his son's murder. While appearing to play-act he kills the murderers in front of

their fathers. 'Ile fit you' seemed to mean, 'I shall cater for your wishes' but the knowingly 'mad' Hieronymo really means, 'I will give you what you deserve'

432 **Datta. Dayadhvam. Damyata** (*Sanskrit*) Give. Sympathise. Control

433 **Shantih shantih shantih** (*Sanskrit*) Eliot, in his note, informs us that the word repeated in this way marks a formal ending to an Upanishad. The Christian equivalent is: 'And the Peace of God, which passeth all understanding, shall keep your hearts and minds through Christ Jesus' (Philippians 4:7)

PART THREE

CRITICAL APPROACHES

STRUCTURE

One of the difficulties most people experience when they read *The Waste Land* for the first time is that they cannot see where the poem is going. The poem appears to belong to none of the main types of English poetry: it is not a narrative or dramatic or descriptive or lyric or meditative poem. These types have characteristic forms of organisation and development but *The Waste Land*, although it manifests certain elements of these types, does not demonstrate an immediately recognisable method of organisation. The reader may find that he or she understands individual lines or even whole sections but does not see how they can fit together. Some critics have gone so far as to deny that *The Waste Land* is a poem at all, and T.S. Eliot himself had serious misgivings about the unity of the work even after he had reduced, with the help of Pound, what he called his 'sprawling chaotic poem'.

Undoubtedly, however, Eliot did have a method according to which he arranged the pieces of his poem. His arrangement or structure has much in common with the work of his contemporary artists in literature and other media (see Background). The parallel most helpful for our present discussion is that of film. A film consists of a sequence of photographs and the sequence is determined by the choice of the director who edits his total collection of photographs into a particular order. He can jump abruptly from one scene to another, introduce shots which go back in time behind the immediate action, even show shots from the future, present the dreams, fantasies and memories of characters. This process of arranging the shots is called 'montage'. In addition, the modern film director can manipulate not just the words of the characters but also sound effects to create atmosphere, evoke memories or arouse expectations. Eliot's method, in *The Waste Land*, of juxtaposing different pieces is very similar to the technique of montage. Such a technique allows the elements of the poem to act on readers in an associative way even though they cannot see, in the initial stages, where they are being led. Gradually, as they read on, certain themes, motifs, tones, even characters begin to develop through repetitions, echoes and similarities. As in an instrumental work of music the main tune or pattern of notes is hinted at, elaborated on and returned to; so, in *The Waste Land*, the central concerns of the poem impress themselves on the reader's mind. There are several ways in which Eliot helps the reader to see the structure of his poem. In the first place, the poem is divided into five parts, each with a title which indicates the focus of the part, and each gathering together material appropriate to that focus. In Part I, Eliot outlines the problem of spiritual deadness. In Part II, he offers two particular examples of the mentality in the waste land which he expands on in Part III where he analyses the perversion of love. Part IV presents an alternative to the death by fire of Part III and indicates that this particular alternative is not a solution to the problem but merely a different sort of ending. In Part V the journey through the waste land is spelled out more clearly than before and the voice of the thunder suggests a remedy to cure the rottenness. This crude summary should not be taken as a description of a straightforward development; *The Waste Land* does not have a tidy plot.

One way in which readers follow the progression in a poem is to attend to the central person involved, be they the narrator or a character: events and situations are seen in terms of this person. In *The Waste Land*, there does not appear to be such a figure. If readers attach themselves to the 'I' in the poem, they quickly discover that the 'I' is not the same person throughout. Eliot, aware of the problem, offers, in his note on line 218, what appears to be a solution. He writes:

> Tiresias, although a mere spectator and not indeed a 'character', is yet the most important personage in the poem, uniting all the rest. Just as the one-eyed merchant, seller of currants, melts into the Phoenician Sailor, and the latter is not wholly distinct from Ferdinand, Prince of Naples, so all the women are one woman, and the two sexes meet in Tiresias. What Tiresias sees, in fact, is the substance of the poem.

This note is helpful in urging readers to dispense with their wish for distinct and realistic characters and in emphasising that there is a mentality prevailing throughout the poem. Readers may well ask, however, how Tiresias is to be distinguished from the author and how, if so many seemingly diverse characters fuse into each other, Tiresias can be said to have any personality at all. During the period when he wrote *The Waste Land* (and the notes), Eliot was concerned that the poet should write impersonally: he, Tom Eliot, should not weep or laugh in a public poem. His note on the role of Tiresias should be taken seriously but not slavishly. The poem is the responsibility of the poet but, it must be stressed, the responsibility of reading the poem falls on the reader and in his or her mind the pieces must cohere. Each part of *The Waste Land* ends with an address to the reader: the hypocrite in Part I, the bystander at Ophelia's mad scene (Part II), the listener to the Fire Sermon (Part III), the voyager in Part IV, and, by implication, still the hypocrite at the end of the poem. The poem's shape and meaning emerge in the reader's mind in so far as he or she is able to grasp them; one has to see 'the substance of the poem'.

A further way in which Eliot helps the reader to see an order in the poem is through his use of **myth**. He acknowledges his debt to Jessie Weston's *From Ritual to Romance* for suggesting 'the title, ... the plan and a good deal of the incidental symbolism of the poem'. It may be that, as with Tiresias, Eliot alleges more than he fulfils but it is true that, throughout the poem, he establishes a network of references to the Grail legend and the vegetation rites closely associated with the legend. Vegetation rites are common to all societies and are so ingrained in the human mind that, even if an individual reader is unacquainted with the stories of the Rhine gold, Thammuz or even the Fisher King, he or she can perceive enough of the fertility network in the poem to give him or her a sense of continuity. The legend of the Grail is further described on page 9.

Two elements in the poem which indicate a pattern are Eliot's use of **allusion** and his **imagery** and these will be discussed in the following pages. In *The Waste Land* they are not easily separable because Eliot takes his inspiration as much from his reading as from his direct experience.

Allusion

An allusion is an indirect reference made to something not immediately under discussion and a literary allusion is the inclusion in the work of one writer of quotations from, or reminders of, the work of another writer.

No author writes in a vacuum and all authors show, in differing degrees, the influence of their reading, but, what the reader encounters in *The Waste Land* is the deliberate incorporation of Eliot's reading. Eliot's own attitude to this practice is made plain in his essays written in the years prior to 1922. In his essay on Philip Massinger (published in *The Sacred Wood*, 1920) he writes:

> Immature poets imitate; mature poets steal; bad poets deface what they take, and good poets make it into something better, or at least something different. The good poet welds his theft into a whole of feeling which is unique, utterly different from that from which it was torn; the bad poet throws it into something which has no cohesion.

He goes so far in 'Tradition and the Individual Talent' (1919) as to propose of the poet that 'we shall often find that not only the best, but the most individual parts of his work may be those in which the dead poets, his ancestors, assert their immortality most vigorously'. In his essay on the Metaphysical Poets in 1921, he develops his point and asserts that:

> Our civilisation comprehends great variety and complexity, and this variety and complexity, playing upon a refined sensibility, must produce various and complex results. The poet must become more and more comprehensive, more allusive, more indirect, in order to force, to dislocate if necessary language into his meaning.

Eliot's concern with a cultural heritage, what he calls 'tradition', is central to all his work. In *The Waste Land* he uses allusions as evidence to show the permanent struggle of humankind to seek or reject truth. His technique, however, poses a number of problems for the reader. In the first place, how essential is it that an allusion be recognised? The answer must be that it varies from allusion to allusion. Some seem self-explanatory in their context in the poem; others seem to have no sense until their original context is known. In both cases, however, knowledge of the original context offers the possibility of a richer sense; otherwise, Eliot would be guilty of confusing the readers by expecting them to exclude from their mind the very associations triggered off by the allusion. The second question raised by the technique is: how much of the original context is being drawn on by the quotation of a single line or even a single word? If Eliot is fully in control of his poem the answer must be that the context in *The Waste Land* helps the reader to determine how much the allusion brings with it from its original context. One example will suffice to illustrate both questions. Line 259 begins 'O City city, …' The reader, arriving at this point, is aware that the City of London is one of the main locations used in the poem and could read line 259 without seeking any further sense or suspecting an allusion. However, the reader might detect a solemnity in this address to the City and might hear a connection between this line and line 257 which, although it is a quotation from Shakespeare's *The Tempest*, links with the biblical line 182, 'By the waters of Leman I sat down and wept'. If these links are heard by the reader, he or she might well be reminded of Jesus weeping over the city of Jerusalem and when he or she consults St Matthew's account finds that Jerusalem, like London, rejects the prophets and their wisdom. This reading of the line, elaborate as it sounds, is supported by the context and by the overall preoccupations of *The Waste Land*.

In the rich and varied allusiveness of the poem it is worth looking at some of the main sources for Eliot's allusions and asking why and how he uses them. The Bible is probably the single most pervasive influence on the poem. Throughout the Bible there is a series of prophetic voices which denounce the way in which the people and their rulers have deserted the true God and pursued false values. From early on (line 19) in *The Waste Land*, Eliot is similarly concerned to expose the decadence and spiritual emptiness of his own time and he invokes the biblical tone and turn of phrase, so recognisable to English speaking readers, to lend authority to his personal vision. Furthermore, the desolation and captivity brought on themselves by the folly of the Israelites offer a parallel to the story of the Fisher King, the Grail and the waste land. This parallel is developed in the obviously Christian element in the legend and by Eliot's introduction of the Hanged Man (Christ) and the journey to Emmaus where the resurrected saviour, sacrificed for the salvation of his people, goes unrecognised.

Dante and Baudelaire are used by Eliot to support his view of the modern city as a condition of horror. Dante's *Hell* and *Purgatory* (significantly, Eliot does not allude to his *Paradise*) are extensions of life and illuminations of it; Baudelaire presents the 'unreal city' directly in his poetry. Both Dante's and Baudelaire's poetry shows an acute awareness of the reader. Eliot harnesses their moral force to confront his reader with the death in life he sees all around him.

The allusions to Wagner's operas are explained in the notes and, for the reader who knows the operas referred to and their legends, the poem is enlarged by these echoes. Eliot is anxious to devise a poem of diverse materials and of wide suggestibility to appeal to different readers. Wagner's operas, exploring the perplexities and aspirations of human beings, themselves draw on their framework of ancient legends and **myths** and Eliot, in alluding to these complex operas, invites the readers to incorporate something of that complexity in their understanding of the poem.

IMAGERY

A poet, when writing of ideas or feelings, must, in order to avoid being too abstract, find terms which suggest the immediate, physical apprehension of these ideas and feelings; such terms are called images. The word '**imagery**' is more generalised and is used to describe the strands of associative language used by a poet. In Shakespeare's play *Hamlet*, for example, there is imagery of corruption and disease running through the play, constantly reminding the reader of the immoral and therefore rotten state of affairs in the court of Denmark.

Imagery of sterility and dryness, appropriate to the condition of the waste land, is evident from the first few lines of the poem where the arrival of spring is viewed with horror by the inhabitants of the 'dead land'. They survive minimally in the 'stony rubbish' (line 20) under a relentless sun. This desert is not in contrast to the 'Unreal City' of line 60 for, in both, the people lack will and vitality. The same symptoms are manifested by the characters of Parts II and III and in the background the rattle of dead bones (lines 116, 186 and 194) mocks the futility and essential deadness of their lives. The desert landscape of Part I reappears in Part V of the poem, in the section considered by Eliot himself to be the best written piece of *The Waste Land*. A change has taken place, however, in that the travellers through the lifeless sand and rock now crave for water and later, when tempted to despair in the 'empty cisterns and exhausted wells' of the ruined chapel, they reassure themselves that 'Dry bones can harm no one'. At the end, with the 'arid plain' behind him, the Fisher King, the ruler and embodiment of the waste land, faces the sea; behind him also are the polluted river and the dull canal, and now the rain intimated by the thunder offers new possibilities in place of the apprehension caused by the spring rain in line 4.

The frailty and corruption of human love is largely presented in images of sexual degradation. Even in the episode of the hyacinth girl with all its marvellous promise there is a sudden inability to communicate, a sense of sexual inadequacy. In a less intense way, the two relationships explored in Part II reiterate the failure of men and women to achieve a partnership of mutual trust and care. The title of Part II, 'A Game of Chess' (see notes and glossary), emphasises the theme of deceit and sexual exploitation and 'The Fire Sermon', concerned as it is with burning, focuses on the fires of sexual lust. The 'sweet Thames' becomes the 'waters of Leman' or prostitution and Eliot is determined to demonstrate how disgusting and depraved men can become in the waste land. Women are reduced to sexual objects for the gratification of lust and they seem to accept tamely the mechanical role they are given to play. Dignity and honour are not considered any longer: 'She smooths her hair with automatic hand,' and, 'What should I resent?'. In the final part, however, in the responses to the voice of the thunder, there is a questioning of the selfish lust which had motivated the characters earlier in the poem; in particular, the sailing image of control and sharing counteracts the images of Philomel, Cleopatra, Dido, Queen Elizabeth and the other women.

A third strand of imagery communicates Eliot's fascination with the transformation of life into death and death into life. At the beginning of the poem the inhabitants of the 'dead land' are barely alive and in line 63, the poet expresses his surprise that 'death had undone so many'. In the final lines of Part I, however, there is some hope offered that the buried corpse may begin to grow. The Egyptian **myth** of Osiris (see note on lines 71–5) symbolised the dying of the land and its rebirth with the rising of the water in the Nile. Throughout the poem there is an uncertainty about the distinction between life and death: corpses can sprout but those who seem to be alive are sometimes 'neither / Living nor dead' (lines 39–40) or are asked, 'Are you alive, or not?' (line 126). This paradox of death in life is seen most acutely in the story of Jesus (lines 328–30) who, as god and man, had lived most fully but appeared to be killed on the cross. Jesus, however, epitomises the myths of the sacrificed but resurrected god of fertility and he reappears to his followers and offers a new life. Earlier in the poem, Eliot cites many examples of transformation in people's lives, some suggesting an improvement, some indicating a deterioration or confusion. Philomel, transformed into a bird, is a plaintive reminder of the brutality of human life. Even Tiresias who has experienced so much as male and female, appears to be, like the Cumaean Sibyl of the epigraph, weary of all behaviour. Phlebas's death by water merely involves him in a repetition of his life: he does not escape from the wheel. However, the references to Ariel's song in Shakespeare's *The Tempest* allow that death by drowning may lead to 'something rich and strange', and St Augustine and the Buddha, when they are rescued from their burning condition, point to a fuller kind of living.

STYLE

Since the poem appeared in 1922, many readers have been impressed with Eliot's versatility in using different verse forms and in varying the tone. Part of his success comes from his competence in mimicking the style of other writers and even incorporating quotations from them; and part also stems from his ability to modulate the pace and seriousness of his poem. In a consideration of the effect of a poem, verse and language cannot, ultimately, be separated but, at this stage, for the sake of brevity and clarity, it is easier to look at each in turn.

VERSE

The lack of a sustained metrical form in *The Waste Land* led some readers to conclude that Eliot had smashed the traditional rules of verse and that he wrote in **free verse**. The poet himself, however, declared that no worthwhile verse can ever be called free because the poet is always in control of his resources. It is true that there is no consistent metre (or pattern of stressed syllables) running through the poem, and the number of syllables in a line varies from one to seventeen; some lines and sections have **rhyme** and others do not; and, in places, Eliot does not use punctuation marks in the conventional way. Nonetheless, he does employ one or more of such devices in different sections of the poem to give an impression of flexible but ordered verse, and it is part of the reader's pleasure in the poem to follow Eliot from the extreme of casual conversation, as in the pub, to the extreme of mechanical nursery rhyme (line 426).

In the opening seven lines of the poem, the basic measure is the line of four stressed syllables but what holds the lines together is Eliot's use of the verbs in the present participle at the end of the lines, sounding like a rhyme, but always needing the next line to complete the sense: a momentum and suspense are created. The following lines sound more casual, a mere sequence of movements, until Marie describes her sled ride and then the short phrases, the alternation of 'we', 'he' and 'I', the repetition of her name, the heavy stress on 'down' (line 16), all contribute to communicate her breathless anxiety.

The first seventeen lines of 'A Game of Chess' consist of two sentences. Rhyme is not used but the stress pattern is reminiscent of Shakespearean **blank verse**. The syntax in both sentences is intricate and the lines run on into the next with the result that the reader has difficulty in keeping control of the sense. This confusion is increased by Eliot's use of past tenses of verbs which can often also serve as adjectives, for example, 'burnished', 'glowed', 'held up', 'wrought', 'fruited' in the first three lines.

A totally different example of Eliot's handling of verse can be seen in the episode concerning the typist (lines 215–56). Rhyme occurs in most of the lines although not according to any rigid scheme. In many of the lines the rhyme on a stressed syllable emphasises the unit of the line and the action of the scene progresses line by line in a mechanical, monotonous way. Sometimes the rhymes are so neat and obvious that they mock the actions; this effect is most noticeable when a shorter word is joined by rhyme with a longer one, for example, 'one bold stare' and 'millionaire', 'defence' and 'indifference', and 'alone' and 'gramophone'.

The description of the journey through the desert in Part V (lines 331–58) has no marks of punctuation and a reading of the passage depends heavily on Eliot's manipulation of the line and his use of repetitions and parallel phrases. 'Water' occurs eleven times, 'rock' nine times, 'mountains' five times and the five conditional clauses beginning with 'if' are answered by five statements beginning with 'but'. The repetitions, the lack of punctuation and the negation emphasise an unending, unprogressing, nightmarish journey; the reader longs for relief, an exit from the labyrinth.

In the course of the poem, Eliot exploits to the full the possibilities of verse based on the stress patterns of conversational English, now tightening, now relaxing the tension. Rhyme is employed to round off a section or emphasise a point. Even in the most casual passages such as the conversation in the pub, the poet formalises the speech by making most lines complete in themselves, repeating 'she said' or 'I said' almost like a rhyme and introducing the refrain, 'Hurry up please it's time'.

LANGUAGE

In the sections on **allusion** and **imagery,** Eliot's choice of language has already been discussed, but something has to be said about his variety of tone and his shifts in vocabulary. *The Waste Land* is a dramatic poem featuring many characters and many scenes. 'He Do the Police in Different Voices', the original title of the poem, offers a clue to Eliot's method of juxtaposing characters and scenes, sometimes for the sake of contrast, more commonly to demonstrate the common fate of all people.

In Part I, after the solemn tone of lines 19–30, derived from the prophetic books of the Bible, Eliot introduces the lyrical intensity of the episode with the hyacinth girl. The man is caught in an emotional paralysis where he can neither speak nor see nor even feel conscious. His condition of helplessness is followed by the description of Madame Sosostris, 'famous clairvoyante'. A clairvoyante is a person who, often in a state of trance, sees what is not present. Madame Sosostris seems to be a direct contrast to the blinded lover but Eliot presents her in such an ironic manner that she emerges as a comic parallel to the man. Her name (see page 16) suggests her bogus status and Eliot immediately undercuts her reputation as a 'famous clairvoyante' by telling the reader that she 'had a bad cold'. In the following lines, with a similar **irony,** 'wisest' is contradicted by 'wicked'.

A similar shift of mood, and tone is apparent in the opening thirty-three lines of 'The Fire Sermon'. Eliot, first of all, presents alongside each other the gentle grace of Spenser's world and the vulgar details of the modern scene. The refrain, 'Sweet Thames, run softly till I end my song' comes to communicate an elegiac mood, a sense of regret. This mood is disrupted by the introduction of 'bones', 'chuckle', 'rat', 'slimy belly' but reappears briefly when the narrator muses on the death of his father and brother. Eliot allows no mood or tone to prevail for long and his lines on Mrs Porter bring an incongruous comic touch to the section. The placing of the French quotation is obviously intended to act in the reader's mind as a comment on Mrs Porter and her crudity, but the pure voices of the children in the chapel are given new words to sing in the lines immediately following.

Such shifts and juxtapositions occur throughout the entire poem: they constitute the texture of the poem. Ornate vocabulary gives way to colloquial dialogue, lyrical moments are interrupted by sordid intrusions, the comic and the macabre coexist with the solemn words of religious instruction, one language is supplanted by another, until in the final lines of the poem the fragments are collected together.

MEANING

Since the poem appeared in 1922 there have been many contradictory reactions to it. Some readers have considered it to be an intellectual puzzle devised for such people as enjoy crossword puzzles. Some have dismissed it as a joke against academic critics and have seen Eliot's notes as his final trick. Some have assessed it as the finest example of **modernist** art, reflecting in its own difficulties the complexity of the modern world. Some have heard in the poem a whimper of despair. Some have sensed that behind the cleverness of the poem a tortured lover was seeking to justify himself. The theories, interpretations and assessments are amazingly diverse and this fact has led some critics to admire a poem that can stimulate so many reactions. Others have been suspicious about a work in which so much is unclear.

Eliot's own comments have not helped to elucidate the problems posed by *The Waste Land,* partly because his own attitude to the poem changed over the years. Originally, readers in the 1920s were encouraged by Eliot's theories of poetry advanced in his essays to believe that the poem was an impersonal object but, later in his life, Eliot described it as a 'wholly insignificant grouse against life; ... a piece of rhythmical grumbling'. In 1932 Eliot wrote:

When I wrote a poem called *The Waste Land* some of the more approving critics
said I had expressed 'the disillusion of a generation', which is nonsense. I may have
expressed for them their own illusion of being disillusioned, but that did not form
part of my intention.

In 1951, however, he asserted that:

A poet may believe that he is expressing only his private experience; his lines may
be for him only a means of talking about himself without giving himself away; yet
for his readers what he has written may come to be the expression both of their
own secret feelings and of the exultation or despair of a generation.

What is undoubtedly clear, whatever Eliot felt he had intended or
disguised, is that certain obsessions, habits of temperament and attitudes
are discernible in the choice of incident and image. Eliot's concern
with blighted sexuality is too persistent to be considered incidental or
contrived: it has the urgency of an unsolved personal problem.

To acknowledge a personal foundation in the poem is not to
undermine the whole construction. The view of life presented in the
poem is narrowed by the peculiar bias of the author but, by fusing his
personal element into the larger story of the Grail and the fertility **myths**
and offering some possibilities beyond his own condition, Eliot succeeds
in persuading the reader that such a view has a wider validity. Mention of
other possibilities raises the question that has vexed critics: does the poem
contain a progression? The first three parts examine the spiritual sickness
of the waste land and in the final part, after the journey to the Chapel of
the Grail is completed, the voice of the thunder offers a diagnosis.
Lacking the capacity to give, one is unable to live in any worthwhile
sense. How can one discover this capacity? Eliot seems uncertain as to
how to proceed. After the commands of the thunder have been
interpreted and the lack of genuine giving has been conceded, the poem
concludes with a series of apparently contradictory statements and the
eventual blessing (see note on line 433). Thus, Eliot does indicate the
direction of a progression and he has shown what has caused the sterility
of the waste land; what he does not present (and it is probable that he
could not at this stage in his life) is a demonstration of a regeneration.
Eliot, like the tormented Hieronymo, understands his situation and can
dare to hope. The reader familiar with the poet's later work, where his
individual regeneration is explored, can see the journey through the waste

land as a hard stage towards the Christian solution he eventually found. Eliot, in *The Waste Land* and his other works, sees the human condition in religious terms and shows little understanding of the economic and social pressures on people. There is little evidence of a sympathetic view of human frailty. Eliot's use of literary **allusion** and ancient myth tends to confirm the opinion that he sees his fellow humans from a distance.

In his critical essays, Eliot asserts that enjoyment precedes interpretation for the reader of poetry. Even for a reader who is antipathetic to what seems to be Eliot's view of his generation or human nature, *The Waste Land* offers a great deal of pleasure. It has proved to be a most memorable poem full of wit, sharp insights, unusual perspective, haunting **rhythms**, suggested depths and sad images of apathy and lovelessness. The poem's enduring popularity and its enormous influence on poets in many languages provide evidence that, for many readers throughout the world, it touches a nerve, it prompts a recognition, it presents, not necessarily *the* truth, but a truth about human failures and aspirations.

PART FOUR

BACKGROUND

LIFE OF T.S. ELIOT

Thomas Stearns Eliot was born in 1888 in Missouri in the United States of America. His father's family traced their ancestors back to immigrants to New England from East Coker, Somerset, in England in the seventeenth century. Eliot's parents were prosperous and cultured and they ensured that he received an excellent education. At Harvard University, where he studied philosophy between 1906 and 1914, Eliot developed an interest in the medieval Italian poet Dante and the nineteenth-century French poets, particularly Baudelaire and Laforgue, and wrote his first significant poems. 'The Love Song of J. Alfred Prufrock', written in 1910–11, was to be the title poem of his first collection of poems published in 1917.

He travelled and studied in France, Germany and England and in 1915 settled in London. After his marriage to an English woman, Vivien Haig-Wood, he worked for a couple of years as a schoolteacher before he obtained a position in Lloyd's Bank. After serving as assistant editor of *The Egoist*, Eliot worked as editor of *The Criterion* from 1922 to 1939; both were influential literary magazines. His second collection of verse, *Poems*, also known as *Ara Vos Prec*, was published in 1920, the date of his first collection of critical essays, *The Sacred Wood*.

Eliot's marriage was not happy and his health deteriorated to such a degree that he had to take an extended holiday first in Margate on the Kent Coast and then in Lausanne in Switzerland. It was during this period that he composed *The Waste Land*, first published in the October 1922 issue of *The Criterion*. In the 1920s Eliot wrote many of his most influential critical essays, particularly on English seventeenth-century literature. *The Hollow Men* appeared in 1925 and by 1930 Eliot had completed *Ash Wednesday* and the *Ariel Poems*. In 1927 Eliot became a British citizen and in 1928 he described his point of view as 'classicist in literature, royalist in politics, and anglo-catholic in religion'. From 1925 till his death, Eliot worked as a director of the publishing company now known as Faber and Faber.

After an absence of seventeen years, Eliot visited the United States to deliver, at Harvard University, lectures published in 1933 as *The Use of Poetry and the Use of Criticism*. In the following year Eliot's pageant play *The Rock* was performed in London. His interest in drama, earlier manifested in the unfinished *Sweeney Agonistes* (1927), developed in the later part of his writing career and he produced five verse plays between 1935 and 1958. *Murder in the Cathedral*, examining the martyrdom of Thomas à Becket, is concerned with similar religious themes to those of *Ash Wednesday*. In *The Family Reunion* (1939), Eliot moves into his contemporary world. The later three plays *The Cocktail Party* (1949), *The Confidential Clerk* (1953), and *The Elder Statesman* (1958), all received their premieres at the Edinburgh Festival and enjoyed considerable commercial success.

In 1935, the year of *Murder in the Cathedral*, Eliot published 'Burnt Norton', the first of his *Four Quartets*, eventually to be completed in 1942. His later work is less cluttered with literary references and demonstrates Eliot's wish to write for a larger audience than that of *The Waste Land*. After 1942 Eliot wrote no poems of significance. The Order of Merit and the Nobel Prize were awarded to him in 1948. In that same year his wife, long since separated from him, died, and in 1957 Eliot married Valerie Fletcher, his secretary. Despite ill health during the final fifteen years of his life, Eliot was able to travel and deliver lectures and his last few years were among his happiest. He died in January 1965 at the age of 76.

INTELLECTUAL BACKGROUND

While at Harvard, Eliot was influenced by the philosopher George Santayana (1863–1952) and the critic Irving Babbitt (1865–1933) who both stressed a need for intellectual self-discipline and the inter-relationship of literary and social values. Santayana and Babbitt could be described as conservative thinkers whereas the British philosopher, F.H. Bradley (1846–1924), the subject of Eliot's doctoral research, was part of a new movement questioning many of the assumptions of nineteenth-century thought. Bradley's *Appearance and Reality* was first published in 1893; in it Bradley declared that most of our statements about the world are 'riddled with contradictions' because we are describing appearance and not reality. When we devise a scientific theory or seek to describe God and the nature of the self we are, according to Bradley, acting without a clear understanding of how the mind perceives the world.

Bradley's challenge formed part of a series of new theories and questions that forced a re-appraisal of traditional attitudes. Back in 1848, Karl Marx (1819–93) and Friedrich Engels (1820–95) had published *The Communist Manifesto*, an analysis of the development of society that emphasised the economic forces which shape social change and the struggle of classes for power. Their attack on what Marx and Engels called capitalist society was not widely supported but, over the following hundred years, Marx's theories and method of social analysis have exerted an enormous influence on the way we think about society and the individual. Furthermore, Marx's view of history is secular and materialistic; as such, it is inevitably in direct conflict with religious belief.

Charles Darwin's (1809–82) book *On the Origin of Species by Means of Natural Selection* appeared in 1859 and offered new evidence in support of an argument challenging the literal truth of the biblical account of mankind's development. Darwin's evolutionary theory suggested that mankind was not created suddenly but was the result of a long development from more primitive forms. Mankind, like other animals, adapts, or is adapted, to function more satisfactorily in an environment. Both Marx's theory of social change, what he called the dialectic, and Darwin's theory of biological evolution shared the idea that mankind was advancing to a better life.

Sigmund Freud (1856–1939), whose work in psychoanalysis began in the 1890s, was fascinated by the primitive in humans, whether in so-called primitive societies or in the unconscious part of the mind. His important work *The Interpretation of Dreams* appeared in 1900. According to Freud, human behaviour is seldom the result of a rational decision but derives from the pressures of our unconscious impulses and fears. Sexual anxiety and the wish for sexual gratification constitute the most dominating force of our lives; our actions are often disguised expressions of this force. In the **imagery** of dreams, **myths** and literature Freud saw the symbolic manifestation of our sexual problems. Throughout his long career, till his death in 1939, Freud conceded that what he was analysing had always been presented by artists but certainly no thinker of the past hundred years has had a more powerful effect on the writer's view of his own work. Freud's one-time colleague, Carl Gustav Jung (1875–1961), saw not sex but a series of mythic patterns, the imprint of the central experiences of mankind, as the basis of our conception of the world. Jung believed that modern humans inherited a store of these mythic patterns, the collective unconscious, and that the artist is a person particularly gifted in bringing these unconscious images, archetypes, to the surface. Freud seemed to see all art as an expression of the artist's disorder or neurosis; Jung saw the artist as the image-maker and spiritual explorer.

Jung and Freud each acknowledged a huge debt to the anthropologist, Sir James Frazer (1854–1941), whose monumental study of primitive ritual and myth, *The Golden Bough*, was published between 1890 and 1915. Frazer's book suggests that no human practice is unique but is one form of response to our shared situation and the similarities between civilised and primitive cultures, between Christianity and pagan religions, are more marked and significant than any contrasts. The idea that human truth and morality make sense in the perspective of a particular tribe and are, therefore, relative has something in common with the theory of relativity worked out for the physical world by the physicist Albert Einstein (1879–1955) at exactly the same period.

This was the period leading up to the First World War (1914–18) in which the European countries that had grown in power during the nineteenth century engaged in a costly and futile struggle. No country emerged from the war stronger or richer, and the main effects of the conflict were a disenchantment with any glib optimism as to the improvement of mankind and a search for some ideology to cope with the economic and political problems of Europe. In 1917 the Russian Revolution under Vladimir Ilyich Lenin (1870–1924) took place and during the early 1920s there was a rapid strengthening of Communist and Fascist parties throughout Europe. The Fascist party led by Benito Mussolini (1883–1945) came to power in Italy in 1922. The basic theoretical difference was that Communism claimed to be government by the people and Fascism claimed that leadership should be given to the people by a select, talented group. In practice both systems seemed to rely on a rigid and exclusive party totally responsible for planning, freedom and justice and both used the army and police to impose a dictatorial system. Artists throughout Europe felt obliged to take sides and many of the major English-speaking writers – W.B. Yeats (1865–1939), Ezra Pound (1885–1972), T.S. Eliot (1888–1965), P. Wyndham Lewis (1884–1957) and D.H. Lawrence (1885–1930) – initially showed sympathy for the Right (the Fascists) against the Left.

A result of the First World War was the break-up of the Austro-Hungarian Empire and its mixture of nationalities and languages. The old aristocratic splendour of Vienna was becoming a thing of the past. It was in the context of this political and ethnic confusion that the German Nazis were later to insist on their idea of racial purity.

Britain, too, was seriously weakened by the war. By the end of the war she had nine million of her citizens in the armed forces and munitions works; she, with her allies from the British Empire, had lost over a million men in the fighting. The Empire itself, the largest the world has seen, was beginning to break apart: there was bitter discontent in areas as far apart as South Africa, Ireland, India and Egypt. In the 1920s the unemployment level rose and many people were forced to live in abject poverty. Over the previous fifty years the provision of education and the organisation of trade unions had improved but it seemed almost impossible for anyone to see a solution to the appalling economic situation after the war. During the nineteenth century there had been a large movement of the British population away from the land and into the rapidly expanding industrial towns. By the 1920s all the major towns and cities had come to include areas of slum conditions. Engines and machines of every sort appeared to be dominating the lives of ordinary people; the people felt that they were becoming parts of a mechanical process. To add to this feeling of helplessness a rigid class structure maintained a system of privilege, snobbery and distrust.

It is curious that such a dismal period should now be referred to as the Roaring Twenties but people did make a hectic attempt to enjoy themselves and to break down the stiff attitudes of Victorian times. Moral codes, traditional Christianity, the roles of the genders, all were challenged and some prominent people made a virtue of shocking and sensational behaviour. The development of radio and film and new, faster methods of travel allowed celebrities to enjoy a previously unprecedented international fame. Newspapers with mass circulations appeared to cultivate in their readers a taste for sensationalism and vulgarity and the most tragic and serious situations were trivialised to cater for this appetite.

The dilemma of America and Europe was one of belief. The seeming solidity of the social class system and orthodox Christian faith so apparent in many aspects of nineteenth-century life was now demonstrated to be inadequate. Friedrich Wilhelm Nietzsche (1844–1900), the German philosopher, had proclaimed that God was dead. The final ten years of his own life till his death in 1900 were spent in physical and mental paralysis; his crude assertion and his paralysis seem deeply symptomatic of intellectual life at the turn of the century. People in the West had exhausted their spiritual supplies; some rushed around looking for replacements in magic, other religions, science, a life of sensations through drugs, sex and excitement, and others claimed that despair was the only honest response to a chaotic universe.

T.S. Eliot, having come from a traditionally minded American background but led by his interests, friendships and reading into the perplexities of the intellectual scene, had to work out his own scheme of beliefs in relation to his personal experiences and the nature of the world around him.

LITERARY BACKGROUND

In the second half of the nineteenth century there were two main movements in European literature: realism and **Symbolism**. The realist writers aimed to present human beings as social creatures, and to lay bare the processes by which economic and political pressures affect their behaviour. In style, the realists sought simplicity, directness, and avoided ornament; accurate representation of a social situation was all important and because of their reformist ideals they often concentrated on the abuses and nastiness in the hope that their readers would feel persuaded to change society. A weakness in the realist writings was the absence of imagination: everything was spelled out clearly and there was little to delight or excite the reader's intellect. This discouragement of imagination, added to the solid social concern, helps to explain why realism had little following among poets and was primarily a movement of novelists and dramatists. It could be argued, however, that realism did help to make some poets more aware of social issues and of a responsibility to their readers, and Walt Whitman (1819–92), the American poet, achieved international fame as a poet of democracy, working people and colloquial language.

Symbolist writing, however, was indirect, **allusive**, often obscure, and tended to concentrate on evoking individual moods and elusive states of mind. The major early symbolist poets were French: Charles Baudelaire (1821–67), Paul Verlaine (1844–96), Arthur Rimbaud (1854–91), Jules Laforgue (1860–87) and Stéphane Mallarmé (1842–98); but their work was not widely known in Britain and America till Arthur Symons (1865–1945) published *The Symbolist Movement in Literature* in 1899. Although these poets often had very decided views on society, the concentration of their poetry was on the processes of their own minds, and fastidious attention was paid to form and language. Words and images were so chosen and arranged as to set up a complex criss-crossing of associations and the reader could delight in exploring this endless maze. Parallel to the realists' emphasis on social injustice and constriction, the symbolists often stressed moods of disappointment, pain, guilt and loneliness. In Baudelaire and Laforgue, however (the symbolists who exerted the strongest influence on Eliot), there is a sense of humour, a mocking self-awareness that helps to balance the private, melancholy quality. Furthermore, in these two poets there is an acute interest in the position of a sensitive, individual artist in a vulgar, materialistic society. In Baudelaire, more than in any other European poet before him, we are made aware of the city with its variety, its crowds, its mechanical cruelty, its excitement, its horror.

In 1908, T.S. Eliot read Symons's *The Symbolist Movement in Literature* and was introduced through it to a kind of poetry that was not being written at that time in America. Curiously enough, one of the major influences on Baudelaire had been the American writer Edgar Allan Poe (1809–49), but Eliot, in his early years, seemed determined to look beyond America for his models and even recent English literature was largely by-passed by him. Indeed, the poetry favoured by him in the preceding period was often the eccentric or idiosyncratic; he declared an admiration for 'The City of Dreadful Night' (1880) by James Thomson (1834–82), and 'Thirty Bob a Week' (1894) by John Davidson (1857–1909), both urban poems, both written by alienated Scotsmen. Robert Browning (1812–89) was an exception to this neglect of English poets and his use of colloquial language and the **dramatic monologue** both influenced Eliot's development. A dramatic monologue is a poem in which we hear the words and thoughts of a character in a situation; the character is not straightforwardly the author, he or she is a dramatic invention of the author.

While he was a student at Harvard, Eliot came to know the work of Dante Alighieri (1265–1321), a poet whom he was later to see as the major guide and model for his own poetry. What Eliot particularly admired in the medieval Italian poet were the directness and economy of his language and the width of emotional experience, especially in the scenes of Hell, Purgatory and Paradise in *The Divine Comedy*. Dante as a figure is present throughout *The Divine Comedy* but, according to Eliot, the reader is not burdened with, or embarrassed by, Dante's private pains or pleasures. Eliot felt that Dante's restraint, his balance between the personal and the impersonal, had much to do with Dante belonging to a tradition of writing and thinking.

During his first ten years in Europe, Eliot spent much of his time considering what he meant by a tradition and attempting to define the tradition of which he felt a part. In 1914 he first met his fellow American poet, Ezra Pound, and they discovered that their poetic interests and aims were very similar. Pound became an indefatigable helper of Eliot, providing him with encouragement, helpful criticism, new ideas, publicity and literary contacts and he made himself responsible for finding publishers for Eliot's poetry. Pound's early poetry, before his major work *The Cantos*, is characterised by a variety of verse forms adapted from many languages and periods. Much of his best work took the form of translations or, more properly, imitations of Classical, medieval Italian and Provençal and Chinese poems. Both Eliot and Pound had learned in their university training to value the achievements of earlier cultural periods and both had developed a gift for selecting a poem, an incident, a person, quintessential to that period. *The Cantos* (1917–69) is Pound's attempt to organise these selections from world history into a vast scheme which could provide an aesthetic, moral and political education for his own generation.

For several years before he met Eliot, Pound was one of the leading

members of the **imagist** group. The imagists felt that poetry in English
had become tired, repetitive and habit-bound; they urged the need for
freedom of subject matter, concentration of statement, originality of
poetic image and the use of a verse free from rigid rules of **rhyme** and
metre. Eliot never belonged to the group but he shared many of their
original aims. Self-discipline, understatement, the inseparability of form
and content were admired by him as classical virtues and he attacked the
expression of unconsidered emotion in stale language that he associated
with the romantic tradition in English poetry.

Many people would now accept the assessment voiced by Eliot and
Pound that English poetry of the late nineteenth and early twentieth
centuries lacked vitality and intellectual rigour. Looking back through the
history of English literature for these missing qualities, Eliot found them
most notably in the work of the poets and dramatists of the first half of
the seventeenth century. In Shakespeare, the group of poets called the
Metaphysical Poets, particularly John Donne (1572–1631), and the
Jacobean playwrights, Eliot discovered a blend of emotion and thought,
immediacy and technical control which, he felt, provided a helpful
example for twentieth-century poets like himself. According to Eliot, a
split between thought and feeling, what he called a '**dissociation of
sensibility**', occurred in English poetry about the time of John Milton
(1608–74) and this split enfeebled nearly all subsequent poets. Before this
split took place, writers saw life whole and the range of vocabulary in their
work reflected the width of this experience and learning; to be
intellectually challenging was for them a virtue and they expected their
readers to enjoy struggling with unusual images, startling juxtapositions,
irony and obliqueness.

Pound and Eliot's questioning of contemporary literary values, their
search for worthwhile models, their experiments with verse, are all part of
a wider European and American development known as **modernism**.
Modernism comprises many divergent theories and movements but all
these are characterised by an overthrow of artistic conventions. For many
members of the public, these movements in music, the visual arts and
literature were not experiments or developments but were insults to the
very idea of art. There were riots in theatres, art galleries and concert
halls; charges of obscenity, irreverence and sensationalism were levelled
against the artists and writers. In 1907 Pablo Picasso (1881–1973)

completed his controversial painting *Les Demoiselles d'Avignon* (The Young Ladies of Avignon). In it the conventional subject of the female nude is dislocated into an arrangement of angular shapes and harsh colours and the faces of several of the young ladies are strongly reminiscent of tribal masks. The result is that the picture can be viewed in different ways: as a variation on a common subject of painting; as a play on geometric patterns; as a cultural or social comment suggesting that behind the present lies the **mythic** or the primitive. Picasso's development lay through cubism which stressed a formalist, abstract element in art, to a collage technique in which various materials and bits and pieces like bottles or metals could be incorporated into a painting in such a way that the traditional gap between the artificial and the actual could be bridged.

The musical event, parallel in its shock effect to Picasso's *Les Demoiselles d'Avignon*, was the performance in 1913 of *The Rite of Spring*, a ballet by Igor Stravinsky (1882–1971). Harsh, strident dissonances interrupted any harmonies and, as in Picasso's composition, the introduction of African-sounding material suggested to the audience a struggle between disorder and order. Eliot saw the ballet performed in London in 1921 and, although he considered that the dancing was not a total success, he felt that the music metamorphosed 'the **rhythm** of the steppes into the scream of the motor horn, the rattle of machinery, the grind of wheels, the beating of iron and steel, the roar of the underground railway, and the other barbaric cries of modern life'. It is apparent that Eliot was impressed not by a clash between ancient ritual and myth and modem behaviour but by a sense of continuity in mankind's search for significance. What was new in Stravinsky was not the presence of ancient myths – Richard Wagner (1813–83) had based his operas on Germanic myths and legends – but the setting of the myth in a modern context and expressed in a modern musical idiom.

Eliot saw that modern life could be interpreted and could gain depth of meaning by being allied to parallel patterns of human behaviour embodied in myth and legend. This idea he saw realised in the work of two of the most distinguished contemporary writers, W.B. Yeats and James Joyce (1882–1941), both Irish. In terms of influence on Eliot's *The Waste Land*, Joyce was the more immediately important figure, so important, indeed, that Eliot told him, 'I wish, for my own sake, that

I had not read it'. The 'it' was Joyce's *Ulysses*, eventually published in Paris in 1922 but parts of which Eliot had been reading as early as 1918. Eliot had come to know Joyce through their mutual friend, Ezra Pound. In *Ulysses*, a single day (16 June, 1904) in the life of Leopold Bloom is presented in detail against a framework of the episodes in the wanderings of Odysseus (Ulysses) in the Greek epic, *The Odyssey*. In its contemporary detail, the novel is highly naturalistic while in its richness of association and cross-reference and in the density of the language it is a **Symbolist** work. Joyce varies the prose style in the different episodes of his novel, ranging from the colloquial to the sophisticated, from passages of dialogue to an unpunctuated stream of consciousness; to describe the style is to offer a catalogue of the experiments in modern literature. In his review of *Ulysses*, Eliot wrote:

> I hold this book to be the most important expression which the present age has found. … In using the myth, in manipulating a continuous parallel between contemporaneity and antiquity, Mr Joyce is pursuing a method which others must pursue after him. … It is simply a way of controlling, of ordering, of giving a shape and significance to the intense panorama of futility and anarchy which is contemporary history.

CRITICAL HISTORY & FURTHER READING

EARLY REACTIONS

When *The Waste Land* appeared in 1922, many of the reviewers declared themselves perplexed. Some attacked the poem as 'waste paper', a 'toad' and even 'a piece of tripe'. There were, however, some very positive reviews, particularly by Edmund Wilson and Conrad Aiken, both of whom grasped and appreciated the poem's disjointed method and allusiveness and comprehended the seriousness of Eliot's subject. Among contemporary American poets there was a common feeling that he, as an American, had betrayed a new vigour apparent in American writing and had written a poem which was heavily European, non-American and largely backward looking. William Carlos Williams described the publication of *The Waste Land* as 'the great catastrophe to our letters' and declared that Eliot had given poetry 'back to the academics'. Hart Crane expressed his disappointment: 'It was good, of course, but so damned dead'; and his disappointment centred on what he saw as its 'complete renunciation' of the world of its time. Ezra Pound, a fellow expatriate, and heavily involved in the shaping and publication of the poem, remained its loudest propagandist. Very quickly, particularly among students and intellectuals, the poem achieved a cult status and its very pessimism was seen as expressing the core mood of the period. By the early 1930s, Eliot's reputation, enhanced by his influential critical essays, was very high on both sides of the Atlantic and the **ironic** complexities of the poetry made him a demonstration piece with the **new critics**. *The Waste Land* was explored and applauded by many of the most regarded critics, including I.A. Richards, William Empson, Robert Graves, Edwin Muir, R.P. Blackmur, F.R. Leavis and Cleanth Brooks. Essays by Leavis and Brooks, in particular, guided the reading of the poem by generations of students; both focused on the **imagery** but Brooks emphasised the **mythic** patterns in Eliot. The first major book devoted to Eliot was F.O. Matthiessen's *The Achievement of T.S. Eliot* (1935) which was subsequently to include discussion of Eliot's later work. W.B. Yeats, the poet of the time with the most established reputation, acknowledged Eliot as 'the most revolutionary man in poetry in my lifetime' but saw him primarily as a satirist who mocked the mechanical quality of urban life.

LATER READINGS

To allocate critics to the categories below is not intended to suggest that all the critics adopt partisan or narrow views of *The Waste Land*. The categories indicate certain emphases in the approaches of different critics.

POLITICAL READINGS

There have always been disagreements concerning the interpretation of the political attitudes in the poem. The poem has been seen as a critique of modern capitalism and an associated lack of humane values: individuality is crushed by the pressures of repetitious work and the conformism of urban living. According to this view, the poem, appearing in the aftermath of the carnage and disillusionment of the First World War, manifested the loss of belief in social progress under the traditional social scheme of things, and Eliot emerged, not as pessimistic, but as a realist. Even in the mid 1930s, a young idealist writer such as John Cornford could feel persuaded to join the Communist Party as a result of his reading of *The Waste Land*. This kind of left-wing acceptance of the poem has become less common as the years have passed and, for many, less tenable, in view of Eliot's own later writings which most readers would see as conservative if not reactionary.

Some readers have always resented what they heard as a superior tone in the poem, a suggestion that ordinary people, people of modern times, are congenitally degraded. Often, for such readers, the method of the poem, its allusiveness, its assumption of competence in several languages, its knowingness, has been part of this superiority, this exclusiveness. Accusations of snobbery made by Philip Rahv in the 1930s were supported by many critics and developed much later in essays by Marxists such as David Craig and Terry Eagleton. Craig's essay, entitled 'The Defeatism of *The Waste Land*' (1960, in Cox and Hinchliffe, 1968), claims that the poem, 'seems to me to work essentially against life, for the range of opinions it mobilises, that come welling up in response to it, are all negative'. Eagleton in his book *Marxism and Literary Criticism* (1976, in Cuddy and Hirsch, 1991) questions Eliot's class awareness, how ideology relates to aesthetic form, and what kind of audience the poem is aimed at. In his work, *Fables of Aggression: Wyndham Lewis, the Modernist as Fascist* (1979), Frederic Jameson identified Eliot as a 'protofascist'. In the 1980s and 1990s, Eliot's political position has come in for severe scrutiny, culminating in Anthony Julius's *T.S. Eliot: Anti-Semitism and Literary Form* (1995), in which his poems, but not particularly *The Waste Land*, are seen to carry anti-Semitic views. A very balanced presentation of Eliot's political position or positions is offered in Michael North's *The Political Aesthetic of Yeats, Eliot and Pound* (1991).

ANTHROPOLOGICAL & RELIGIOUS READINGS

In his general note on the poem, Eliot acknowledges a debt to the work of the anthropologists, Jessie L. Weston and Sir James Frazer. This acknowledgement has led many readers to seek in these authors for the meaning of the poem but many readers have emerged from Weston and Frazer without finding the desired clarification. Cleanth Brooks's influential essay '*The Waste Land*: Critique of the Myth' (1939, in Cox and Hinchliffe, 1968) has helped to show how the poem is organised round certain mythic schemes, and his essay opened out ideas of fertility rituals and parallelism between aspects of the modern world and 'primitive' myths. These anthropological and mythic aspects of the poem have been widely explored in the work of such critics as Northrop Frye, Helen Gardner, Grover Smith, Robert Crawford and Cleo McNelly Kearns. Discussion of myth leads to discussion of belief and religion. Various critics, including some of those just named, have tried to ascertain whether or not Eliot offers through *The Waste Land* some cohesive religious or specifically Christian position. His use of biblical material has been focused on by some, but the references to Indian religions have to be accommodated. There is a measure of agreement among critics that the poem raises religious questions but does not advance any clear religious answer.

BIOGRAPHICAL READINGS

Because Eliot was such a discreet and private individual and because in his critical essays he emphasised a separation between the poet and the poem, early discussion of the poem did tend to focus on *The Waste Land* as a text detached from its author. Furthermore, Eliot resisted enquiries into his personal life and left instructions with his widow to give no encouragement to any putative biographer. In 1952 John Peter wrote an essay, 'A New Interpretation of *The Waste Land*' (published in *Essays in Criticism*) but was forced by Eliot with threats of legal action to withdraw the article. Peter read the poem as an **elegy** for a lost homosexual love. In 1984 Peter Ackroyd published a biography, *T.S. Eliot*, but was 'forbidden by the Eliot estate to quote from Eliot's published work, except for purposes of fair comment in a critical context, or to quote from Eliot's unpublished work or correspondence'. Some years before Ackroyd wrote his book, surprisingly good considering the difficult circumstances in which it was written, Lyndall Gordon brought out *Eliot's Early Years* (1977) with what looked like the tacit agreement of Eliot's widow. These three biographical forays present Eliot, at the time of writing *The Waste Land*, as a deeply troubled person, unsure of what he could believe in or trust, unconfident in his relationships and ambivalent about his sexual feelings. Something of this fundamental perplexity is central to the poem and gives an emotional urgency and immediacy to what might otherwise seem a mere 'heap of broken images'. In his essay '*The Waste Land*: The Prison and the Key' (1974, in Moody, 1974), Richard Drain examines the poem as a work of 'the isolated sensibility', a work in which Eliot explores the prison of himself. Ronald Schuchard offers an insight into Eliot's horror in a chapter on *The Waste Land* in his book, *Eliot's Dark Angel: Intersections of Life and Art* (1999).

LITERARY READINGS

Eliot's own views on the practice of criticism are largely consistent across his career. He writes: 'The ideal critic ... should not be primarily concerned with sociology, or with psychology, or with politics, or with theology, or with any other ology; he should be primarily concerned with the word and the incantation'. His identification with the **new critics** from the 1930s to the 1950s ensured that some of these critics would concentrate on how *The Waste Land* works as a poem. I.A. Richards, F.R. Leavis and Cleanth Brooks followed this approach. Not all critics, however, who looked at the poem as a poem came to the same estimation of the poem's success. Graham Hough in his essay 'Imagism and Its Consequences' (1960, in Bloom, 1986) offers a fierce scrutiny of how *The Waste Land* works, taking as a starting point Eliot's own theory of the **objective correlative**. Kathleen Nott in her essay 'Ideology and Poetry' (1974, in Moody, 1974) again questions how coherent the poem is and, although she enjoys the performance in the poem, concludes that Eliot's ideas, particularly of the Tradition, do not work convincingly. In 'The Structure and Mythical Method of *The Waste Land*' (1983, in Cuddy and Hirsch, 1991), Grover Smith re-examines the very method claimed by Eliot, the 'mythic method' learned from his reading of Joyce's *Ulysses*, and finds that the method does not entirely succeed. These three essays by Hough, Nott and Smith do examine how the poetry functions and they all base themselves on one of Eliot's own theories about how the poem works. Ronald Bush in his essay, 'T.S. Eliot and Modernism at the Present Time: A Provocation' (1991, in Bush, 1991) takes Eliot into the challenge of **postmodernism** but, although he acknowledges that some more recent writings on *The Waste Land* are 'more subtle and better informed' than earlier criticism, the view of the poem is not clearer and the poetry survives attempts at its deconstruction. The very uncertainties, ambivalence and self-questioning **ironies** of the poem seem to anticipate later developments in literary theory.

FURTHER READING

TEXT OF THE POEM

T.S. Eliot, *The Complete Poems and Plays of T.S. Eliot*, Faber and Faber, London, 1969

Valerie Eliot, (ed.), *The Waste Land: A Facsimile and Transcripts of the Original Drafts*, Faber and Faber, London, 1971

OTHER WORKS BY T.S. ELIOT

T.S. Eliot, *Selected Essays*, third edition, Faber and Faber, London, 1951

Particularly recommended are the essays: 'Tradition and the Individual Talent' (1919); *Hamlet* (1919); 'Philip Massinger' (1920); 'The Metaphysical Poets' (1921); 'Andrew Marvell' (1921);'Dante' (1929); and 'Baudelaire' (1930)

Frank Kermode, (ed.), *Selected Prose of T.S. Eliot*, Faber and Faber, 1975

Wider selection than Eliot's own choice but shorter

Valerie Eliot, (ed.), *The Letters of T.S. Eliot*, vol. I: 1898–1922, Faber and Faber, 1988

BOOKS ON T.S. ELIOT

F.O. Matthiessen, *The Achievement of T.S. Eliot* (first edition 1935), third edition, Oxford University Press, 1958

Intelligent and sympathetic early study. Presents Eliot in his American context

C.K. Stead, *The New Poetic*, Hutchison, 1964

Explores Eliot's poetic theories and relates him to developments in modern poetry

Herbert Howarth, *Notes on Some Figures Behind T.S. Eliot*, Chatto and Windus, 1965

Informative, particularly on the poet's education and reading

Stephen Spender, *Eliot*, Collins/Fontana, 1975

Readable, succinct and comprehensive study by a poet who knew Eliot

Lyndall Gordon, *Eliot's Early Years*, Oxford University Press, 1977

Short, informative biography on aspects of Eliot's earlier life and work (including *The Waste Land*)

Peter Ackroyd, *T.S. Eliot*, Hamish Hamilton, 1984

Excellent, wide-ranging and questioning biography, closely relating the life to the work

Robert Crawford, *The Savage and the City in the Work of T.S. Eliot*, Clarendon Press, 1987

Relates Eliot to the anthropological, genetic and sociological theories of his time

Ronald Bush, (ed.), *T.S. Eliot: The Modernist in History*, Cambridge University Press, 1991

> Includes essays on feminist aspects by Lyndall Gordon and Carol Christ, a fascinating account of the publishing of *The Waste Land* and sharp essays by Michael North and Ronald Bush

Michael North, *The Political Aesthetic of Yeats, Eliot and Pound*, Cambridge University Press, 1991

> Strong, balanced section on political elements in Eliot, including *The Waste Land*

A. David Moody, (ed.), *Cambridge Companion to T.S. Eliot*, Cambridge University Press, 1994

> Contains essays on biography, philosophy, tradition, literary theory in relation to Eliot's work

Anthony Julius, *T.S. Eliot: Anti-Semitism and Literary Form*, Cambridge University Press, 1995

> Rigorous interrogation of Eliot's views on Semitism and related subjects

Ronald Schuchard, *Eliot's Dark Angel: Intersectons of Life and Art*, Oxford University Press, 1999

> Densely argued presentation of Eliot's work in relation to his emotional life

BOOKS ON *THE WASTE LAND*

C.B. Cox and Arnold Hinchliffe, (eds), *T.S. Eliot: The Waste Land*, Macmillan, London, 1968

> Includes comments by Eliot, early reviews, passages from Richards, Empson, Winters and essays by Aiken, Wilson, Brooks, Kenner and Craig

M.C. Bradbrook, *T.S. Eliot: The Making of The Waste Land*, Longman, 1972

> Short detailed examination of the manuscripts and typescripts that became the poem

Helen Williams, *T.S. Eliot: The Waste Land*, second edition, Edward Arnold, 1973

> Short but detailed analysis of the poem, testing several interpretative approaches

A.D. Moody, (ed.), *The Waste Land in Different Voices*, Edward Arnold, 1974
> Selection of essays on the poem including ones by Drain and Nott

Stephen Coote, *The Waste Land*, Penguin Books, 1985
> Chapters on aspects of the poem. Substantial investigation into the sources of the poem

Harold Bloom, (ed.), *T.S. Eliot's The Waste Land*, Chelsea House Publishers, 1986
> Includes essays by Bloom, Hough, Grover Smith, Cleo McNelly, Kearns

Lois A. Cuddy and David H. Hirsch, (eds), *Critical Essays on T.S. Eliot's The Waste Land*, G.K. Hall and Company, 1991
> Contains some early reviews, articles on the publishing history of the poem, and articles by a wide range of critics including Richards, Blackmur, Rahv, Brooks, Grover Smith, Frye, Eagleton, Eloise Knapp Hay

John Peter, 'A new interpretation of *The Waste Land*', *Essays in Criticism*, ii, July 1953, pp. 242–66; reprinted in *Essays in Criticism*, XIX, Spring 1969, pp. 140–75.

World events	Author's life	Cultural events
	1670 (c) Andrew Eliot, ancestor of TS Eliot, emigrates from East Coker, Somerset to Massachusetts	
1865 End of American Civil War		
		1876 Wagner, *The Ring* completed
		1880 Dostoevsky, *The Brothers Karamazov*
		1883 Nietzsche, *Thus Spake Zarathustra*
		1886 Henry James, *The Bostonians*
		1887 Mallarmé, *Poems*
	1888 Thomas Stearns Eliot born in St Louis, youngest of seven children	
		1889 Death of Browning, Hopkins
		1890 Frazer, *The Golden Bough*, vol 1 (-1915)
		1891 Ibsen, *Ghosts* performed in London
		1892 Death of Whitman, Tennyson; Kipling, *Barrack-Room Ballads*
		1893 Yeats, *The Celtic Twilight*; Dvorak, Symphony 5 ('from the New World'); Munch, *The Cry*
		1894 Sibelius, *Finlandia*
1896 Gold Rush in Klondike		
		1898 Wells, *War of the Worlds*
1899 War between British and Boers in South Africa (till 1902)		**1899** Wilde, *The Importance of Being Earnest*
1900 Boxer Riots in China		**1900** Freud, *The Interpretation of Dreams*; Conrad, *Heart of Darkness*

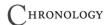

World events	Author's life	Cultural events
1901 Queen Victoria dies; Theodore Roosevelt becomes President of USA		
		1902 William James, *The Varieties of Religious Experience*
1903 Henry Ford sets up Ford Motor Company; Wright brothers make first flight in heavier-than-air machine		**1903** London, *The Call of the Wild*
		1904 Conrad, *Nostromo;* Chekhov, *The Cherry Orchard*
1905 First underground lines and motor buses in London		**1905** Marinetti, *Futurist Manifesto;* Strauss, *Salomé*
1906 Major earthquake in San Francisco	**1906-10** Studies at Harvard, publishes poems in college magazine	
		1907 Synge, *The Playboy of the Western World;* Picasso, *Desmoiselles d'Avignon*
1908 Massive earthquake in Southern Italy		
		1909 Matisse, *The Dance;* Ballet Russe under Diaghilev appears in Paris
	1910 Studies in Paris	**1910** Post-Impressionist Exhibition in London
	1910-12 Writes 'Preludes', 'Prufrock', 'Rhapsody on a Windy Night', 'Portrait of A Lady', 'La Figlia che Piange'	
	1911-14 Takes courses in Indian Philosophy and works on his doctoral thesis in Philosophy	
1912 London by now has 400 cinemas; Woolworths Stores open; Titanic sinks		

World events	Author's life	Cultural events
1913 Gandhi arrested for his campaign of resistance to British rule in India		**1913** Lawrence, *Sons and Lovers;* Mann, *Death in Venice;* Proust, first volume of *A la Recherche du Temps Perdu;* Frost, *A Boy's Will;* Armory Show of modern art in New York; Stravinsky, *Rite of Spring* in Paris
1914 First World War begins; Panama Canal opens	**1914** Studies in Germany and Oxford; meets Ezra Pound and Bertrand Russell	**1914** Joyce, *Dubliners;* Yeats, *Responsibilities;* Frost, *North of Boston;* Hardy, *Satires of Circumstance;* Lindsay, *The Congo and Other Poems*
1915 German airships bomb English ports; Lusitania is sunk by German submarine	**1915** Marries Vivian Haigh-Wood, works as school-teacher	**1915** Buchan, *The Thirty-Nine Steps;* Pound, *Cathay;* Brooke (died 1914), *1914 and Other Poems;* Masters, *Spoon River Anthology;* Griffith, *Birth of a Nation*
1916 Battles of Verdun and Somme lead to huge casualties; Easter Rising in Dublin against British rule	**1916** Finishes his thesis for Harvard but does not go to America to complete the formalities for his doctorate; begins writing reviews for journals, teaches evening classes	**1916** Joyce, *A Portrait of the Artist as a Young man;* Sandburg, *Chicago Poems*
1917 Russian Revolution; US enters war against Germany	**1917** Begins to work in Lloyds Bank; publishes *Prufrock and other Observations*	**1917** Jung, *Psychology of the Unconscious;* Thomas (died 1917), *Poems*
1918 First World War ends with defeat of Germany; influenza epidemic kills over twenty million people		**1918** Hopkins (died 1889), *Poems* Spengler, *Decline of the West,* vol 1 (-1922)
1919 League of Nations established in Paris; civil war in Russia; Alcock and Brown fly across the Atlantic; Treaty of Versailles recognises break-up of Austro-Hungarian Empire	**1919** Father dies; publishes 'Tradition and the Individual Talent' in *The Egoist,* a periodical he helps to edit	

Chronology

World events	Author's life	Cultural events
1920 Massive earthquake in China; Sacco and Vanzetta in US accused as anarchists and indicted for murder (executed 1927); prohibition introduced in US	**1920** *The Sacred Wood* (critical essays) and *Poems* (including 'Gerontion') published; visits Joyce in Paris; begins work on what is to emerge as *The Waste Land*	**1920** Owen (died 1918), *Poems;* Valéry, *Le Cimetière Marin;* Holst, *The Planets;* Pound, *Hugh Selwyn Mauberley*
1921 BBC founded	**1921** Suffers a mental breakdown, recuperates in Margate, attends psychiatrist in Lausanne; hands over his *Waste Land* drafts to Pound	**1921** Pirandello, *Six Characters in Search of an Author;* Chaplin, *The Kid*
1922 Hunger marches in Britain; Civil War in newly established Free State of Ireland; Mussolini leads Fascist march on Rome; tomb of Pharaoh Tutan Khamun excavated in Egypt; Marie Stopes holds meetings advocating birth control	**1922** *The Waste Land* published in *The Criterion* (new periodical, edited by Eliot till 1939), *The Dial,* and as a book with notes	**1922** Joyce, *Ulysses;* Brecht, *Baal;* Mansfield, *The Garden Party;* O'Neill, *The Hairy Ape;* Sitwell, *Façade;* Marie Lloyd dies
		1923 Williams, *Spring and All;* Stevens, *Harmonium;* Frost, *New Hampshire;* Lawrence, *Birds, Beasts and Flowers;* Nobel Prize to Yeats; Gershwin, *Rhapsody in Blue;* Rilke, *Duino Elegies;* ee cummings, *Tulips and Chimneys*
1924 Death of Lenin		**1924** Forster, *Passage to India;* Death of Kafka, FH Bradley; Mann, *The Magic Mountain;* O'Casey, *Juno and the Paycock;* Wodehouse, *Jeeves*

World events	Author's life	Cultural events
1925 First television images transmitted; Scopes trial in Tennessee bans the teaching of Darwinian theory of evolution	**1925** Published *Poems, 1909-25* (including 'The Hollow Men'); leaves his work in bank and joins publishing company Faber and Gwyer (later Faber and Faber)	**1925** Fitzgerald, *The Great Gatsby;* Eisenstein, *The Battleship Potemkin;* Chaplin, *The Gold Rush;* Berg, *Wozzeck;* Pound, *A Draft of XVI Cantos*
1926 General Strike in Britain		**1926** Kafka, *The Castle;* Tawney, *Religion and the Rise of Capitalism;* Lang, *Metropolis;* MacDiarmid, *A Drunk Man Looks at the Thistle;* Jeffers, *Roan Stallion, Tamar, and Other Poems*
1927 General financial collapse in Germany	**1927** Becomes a British citizen and a member of the Church of England; publishes 'Journey of the Magi'	**1927** Hesse, *Steppenwolf;* Woolf, *To the Lighthouse;* Pavlov, *Conditioned Reflexes*
1928 Women's voting age in Britain reduced from 30 to 21	**1928** Publishes *For Lancelot Andrewes* (critical essays)	**1928** Yeats, *The Tower;* death of Hardy; Disney, first Mickey Mouse film
1929 Labour Government re-elected; 'Black Friday' stock exchange crash on Wall Street, New York has worldwide effects		**1929** Faulkner, *The Sound and the Fury;* Second *Surrealist Manifesto*
	1930 Publishes *Ash Wednesday*	**1930** Crane, *The Bridge;* Auden, *Poems;* Freud, *Civilisation and its Discontents;* Keynes, *Treatise on Money*
1931 Nearly three million unemployed in Britain.		**1931** Dali, *Persistence of Memory;* Epstein, *Genesis*
	1932 Visits America to deliver series of lectures at Harvard and University of Virginia; *Selected Essays 1917-1932* published	**1932** Huxley, *Brave New World;* Bergson, *Two Sources of Morality and Religion;* Leavis, *New Bearings in English Poetry*

World events	Author's life	Cultural events
1933 Hitler becomes Chancellor of Germany; first concentration camp in Germany; burning of 'decadent' books; 92% of electorate votes for Nazi Party	**1933** Returns from America; separates from his wife who has suffered severe mental problems during their relationship; *The Use of Poetry and The Use of Criticism* (lectures given at Harvard) published	**1933** Jung, *Modern Man in Search of his Soul*
1934 Mao Tse-tung begins the Long March across China		
1935 Germany re-arms; legislation against Jews; Italy invades Abyssinia	**1935** *Murder in the Cathedral* performed in Canterbury	**1935** Odets, *Waiting for Lefty;* Epstein, *Ecce Homo*
1936 Spanish Civil War begins; Mosley and his Fascists try to march through the East End of London; Edward VIII abdicates; unemployed shipyard workers march to London from the north east of England; Olympic Games held in Berlin	**1936** *Collected Poems, 1909-35* (includes 'Burnt Norton')	**1936** Huxley, *Eyeless in Gaza;* Thomas, *Twenty-Five Poems;* Chaplin, *Modern Times;* Auden, *Look, Stranger!;* Penguin Books begin production
1937 German bombers destroy Guernica in Spain		**1937** Jones, *In Parenthesis;* Stevens, *The Man with the Blue Guitar;* Muir, *Journeys and Places;* Picasso, *Guernica*
1938 Germany annexes Austria		**1938** Auden and Isherwood, *On the Frontier;* Wilder, *Our Town;* Sartre, *Nausea;* Greene, *Brighton Rock*
1939 Germany and USSR sign non-aggression pact; Germany invades Czechoslovakia, then Poland; Britain declares war; Nationalists under Franco defeat Republicans in Spain	**1939** *The Family Reunion* performed; publishes *The Idea of a Christian Society* (lectures) and *Old Possum's Book of Practical Cats*	**1939** MacNeice, *Autumn Journal;* Joyce, *Finnegans Wake; Gone with the Wind* (film); Yeats dies

World events	Author's life	Cultural events
1940 Churchill replaces Chamberlain as Prime Minister; evacuation of British troops from Dunkirk; Battle of Britain; blitz attacks on London and other cities; Japan joins alliance of Germany and Italy	**1940** Part-time fire watcher during the air raids on London; publishes 'East Coker'	**1940** Koestler, *Darkness at Noon*
1941 Germany invades USSR; Japan bombs US fleet at Pearl Harbour; US joins in the war	**1941** Publishes 'Dry Salvages'	**1941** Orson Welles, *Citizen Kane;* Joyce dies
1942 Singapore falls to the Japanese; defeat of German army in North Africa	**1942** Publishes 'Little Gidding'	
1943 Surrender of German army to Russians at Stalingrad	**1943** Publishes *Four Quartets*	**1943** Sartre, *Being and Nothingness;* Brecht, *The Good Woman of Setzuan; Life of Galileo*
1945 Surrender of Germany to the Allies; suicide of Hitler; trial of Nazi leaders begins at Nuremberg; Atlee wins British election; United Nations Organisation is set up		**1945** Orwell, *Animal Farm*
	1946 Travels to America, visits Ezra Pound	
1947 Partition of Indian sub-continent into India and Pakistan	**1947** Honorary Degrees from Harvard, Princeton, Yale; his wife Vivien dies	**1947** Williams, *A Streetcar Named Desire*
1948 Palestine is declared the Jewish state of Israel; Gandhi is assassinated	**1948** Awarded Order of Merit and Nobel Prize for Literature; publishes *Notes Towards the Definition of Culture*	
1949 Communist rule is established in China	**1949** *The Cocktail Party* performed at Edinburgh Festival	**1949** Pound, *Pisan Cantos; Miller, Death of a Salesman; Orwell, Nineteen Eighty-Four*
1950 Korean War begins		

Y

CHRONOLOGY

World events	Author's life	Cultural events
	1951 Suffers a mild heart attack resulting in poor health for the remainder of his life	
1953 Coronation of Queen Elizabeth; death of Stalin;	**1953** *The Confidential Clerk* performed at Edinburgh Festival	**1953** Beckett, *Waiting for Godot* in Paris
1956 The Suez Crisis; Soviet Union crushes revolt in Hungary		**1956** Osborne, *Look Back in Anger;* Ginsberg, *Howl*
1957 Soviet sputniks launched	**1957** Marries his secretary, Valerie Fletcher; *On Poetry and Poets* published	**1957** Smith, *Not Waving but Drowning;* Hughes, *Hawk in the Rain;* Gunn, *Sense of Movement*
	1958 *The Elder Statesman* performed at Edinburgh Festival	
1959 Castro becomes leader in Cuba		**1959** Lowell, *Life Studies*
1960 John F. Kennedy becomes US President; Civil War in Congo; massacre at Sharpeville in South Africa		**1960** Betjemann, *Summoned by Bells;* Plath, *The Colossus;* Pinter, *The Caretaker*
1961 Berlin Wall is built		**1961** Heller, *Catch-22*
1962 Missile crisis over Cuba; second Vatican Council meets; end of military service in Britain		**1962** Britten, *War Requiem;* Burgess,*A Clockwork Orange;* Albee, *Who's Afraid of Virginia Woolf?*
1963 President Kennedy is assassinated	**1963** Visits America for the last time; *Collected Poems 1909-1962* published	**1963** Plath commits suicide
1964 Krushchev is removed from power; Harold Wilson becomes Prime Minister; US becomes more involved in war in Vietnam		**1964** Lowell, *For the Union Dead;* Ginsberg, *Kaddish and Other Poems*
1965 Churchill dies; Rhodesia declares its independence	**1965** Dies in London and his ashes interred in the parish church at East Coker	**1965** Plath, *Ariel*
		1966 Heaney, *Death of a Naturalist*

alliteration the repetition of consonantal sounds (usually at the beginning of a word, and often in successive words) in a piece of writing

allusion a reference in a work of literature to something outside itself. Literary allusion involves the quotation of, or reference to, another literary text. Depending on the context in which the allusion is included, the effect may be one of comparison, contrast or irony

assonance the use of the same vowel sounds with different consonants in successive words or stressed syllables e.g. nation and traitor

blank verse unrhymed iambic pentameter: a line of, on average, five main stresses, ten syllables. It is the main verse form of Shakespeare's plays and Milton's *Paradise Lost*

dramatic monologue poem in which a single persona, not the poet, is speaking to a person or persons whose presence is implied. In some cases, a helpful comparison would be that, for the reader, it is like listening to one side of a telephone conversation. Famous examples include Burns's 'Holy Willie's Prayer', Tennyson's 'Ulysses', Browning's 'My Last Duchess' and Eliot's 'The Love Song of J. Alfred Prufrock'

dissociation of sensibility a phrase coined by Eliot in his essay on 'The Metaphysical Poets' (1921). Eliot claimed that in the earlier seventeenth century poets enjoyed a unified sensibility in which thoughts and feelings were often interchangeable. According to Eliot, towards the end of the century, partly under the influence of Milton and Dryden, thought came to be separated from feeling and this dissociation weakened most of the poetry written between then and Eliot's own time

elegy a poem of lamentation, concentrating on the death of an admired or loved figure

free verse verse written without the constraints of conventional metre and rhyme It is printed in irregular lines (not continuously like prose) and the lineation is a major element in it. Rhythm may be obvious in places but not becoming as predictable as metre. The word 'free' is misleading, according to some of the major practitioners such as W.C. Williams, Pound and Eliot; it requires its own particular discipline

imagery all the words that refer to objects and qualities which appeal to the senses and feelings. In presenting themes in terms of particular imagery, authors show their attitudes to these themes. For example, Eliot in *The Waste Land* tends to present human love in terms of sterility, boredom, impotence and sordidness; repeated kinds of imagery reinforce an atmosphere or way of thinking

imagism a movement among poets in America and Britain between roughly 1910 and 1920 which wished to prune away much of the opinions, wordiness and decoration from the poetry of the turn of the century. Pound, T.E. Hulme, Amy Lowell were leading figures and it had considerable influence on poets as different from each other as W.C. Williams and Eliot. Imagism's insistence on brevity limited its suitably for more ambitious poets and its impact receded in the 1920s

irony a way of writing (or speaking) in which what seems to be said is different from what is intended. The reader often needs to reread the passage in order to ascertain the presence of irony. Irony requires a context in which to operate, and entails a complicity between the author and the reader

metaphor a figure of speech in which a word or phrase is applied to an object or action that it does not literally denote in order to imply a resemblance

modernism an artistic movement in the early part of the twentieth century which was self-consciously in revolt against certain conventions of the late nineteenth century and innovative in its own practice. The boundaries of what could be called 'art' were challenged, and in formal arrangement as well as subject matter an element of shock or disruption was crucial. In music, the visual arts and literature, and in mixtures of them, an emphasis was placed on discordance at the same time as large subjects were explored. The very ambition and demand for originality behind modernism became tiring to the artists and tiresome to the public

myth stories, usually concerning superhuman heroes or gods, which describe or explain religious beliefs. Tribal societies have myths of creation, disasters, good fortune, and death; and human beings have their place in a larger scheme of the natural world, the universe, and the powers which operate the scheme. In recent criticism, 'myth' is used to describe the complete range of systems and signs by which a society expresses its cultural values

new criticism a critical movement prominent in the United States in the 1930s through to the 1950s and influential well beyond the mid-century in the teaching of literature particularly in English. The new critics recommended that a poem (and they focused on poetry) should be studied as a poem, a special construction of words, and not as a piece of biographical, historical or sociological evidence.

Close reading of texts should, according to the new critics, reveal how a text functions and lead towards some kind of consensus about interpretation

objective correlative term coined by Eliot in his essay 'Hamlet and His Problems' (1919) to describe how an author cannot convey emotion directly to the reader but must find a satisfactory equivalent in, for example, actions or images which can stand for the emotion and prompt the appropriate response in the reader

persona a character devised in such a way that the author can, through that character's voice, explore certain situations or emotions (see dramatic monologue)

postmodernism the term is very vague but has two main areas of meaning. First, it is often used to describe various kinds of writing and criticism after the dominant period of modernism. Second, it describes a variety of critical approaches united in challenging the idea that a word or a text can have a single, undisputed meaning. The author is denied any proprietorial or exclusive claim to the interpretation of his or her writing. All language is slippery and subject to a plurality of readings according to circumstances and the changing viewpoint of different readers

rhyme chiming or matching sounds which create a very clearly audible sense of pattern

rhythm the chief element of rhythm is the variation in levels of stress accorded to the syllables

Symbolism this term has to be distinguished from 'symbolism' without a capital. The Symbolist (in French, Symboliste) movement was particularly strong in France in the second half of the nineteenth century and involved poets such as Baudelaire, Rimbaud, Verlaine, Laforgue and Mallarmé. The central belief of the movement was that there is a correspondence between the internal (the mind) and the external (the world) and between the natural realm and the spiritual, and that language or colour or sounds can mediate between these areas. This spiritual belief and the art it engendered exercised a strong influence on some modernist poets such as Eliot, Valéry, Yeats, and, later, Sorley MacLean. Eliot, however, was less persuaded of the belief and more attracted by some of the social poetry of Baudelaire and Laforgue

AUTHOR OF THIS NOTE

Alasdair D.F. Macrae was educated at the University of Edinburgh and taught for a short time in secondary schools before taking up a lectureship in the University of Khartoum, Republic of the Sudan. He became lecturer in English Studies at the University of Stirling and subsequently Senior Lecturer. He has published widely mainly on modern poetry, including essays on W.B. Yeats, Seamus Heaney, Les Murray, Norman MacCaig, Edwin Muir. *Shelley: Selected Poetry and Prose* was published in 1991; *W.B. Yeats: A Literary Life* was published in 1995. Alasdair is currently engaged in research on Inhumanism and Modern Poetry.

York Notes Advanced

Margaret Atwood
Cat's Eye

Margaret Atwood
The Handmaid's Tale

Jane Austen
Emma

Jane Austen
Mansfield Park

Jane Austen
Persuasion

Jane Austen
Pride and Prejudice

Jane Austen
Sense and Sensibility

Alan Bennett
Talking Heads

William Blake
Songs of Innocence and of Experience

Charlotte Brontë
Jane Eyre

Charlotte Brontë
Villette

Emily Brontë
Wuthering Heights

Angela Carter
Nights at the Circus

Geoffrey Chaucer
The Franklin's Prologue and Tale

Geoffrey Chaucer
The Miller's Prologue and Tale

Geoffrey Chaucer
Prologue To the Canterbury Tales

Geoffrey Chaucer
The Wife of Bath's Prologue and Tale

Samuel Taylor Coleridge
Selected Poems

Joseph Conrad
Heart of Darkness

Daniel Defoe
Moll Flanders

Charles Dickens
Bleak House

Charles Dickens
Great Expectations

Charles Dickens
Hard Times

Emily Dickinson
Selected Poems

John Donne
Selected Poems

Carol Ann Duffy
Selected Poems

George Eliot
Middlemarch

George Eliot
The Mill on the Floss

T.S. Eliot
Selected Poems

T.S. Eliot
The Waste Land

F. Scott Fitzgerald
The Great Gatsby

E.M. Forster
A Passage to India

Brian Friel
Translations

Thomas Hardy
Jude the Obscure

Thomas Hardy
The Mayor of Casterbridge

Thomas Hardy
The Return of the Native

Thomas Hardy
Selected Poems

Thomas Hardy
Tess of the d'Urbervilles

Seamus Heaney
Selected Poems from Opened Ground

Nathaniel Hawthorne
The Scarlet Letter

Homer
The Iliad

Homer
The Odyssey

Aldous Huxley
Brave New World

Kazuo Ishiguro
The Remains of the Day

Ben Jonson
The Alchemist

James Joyce
Dubliners

John Keats
Selected Poems

Christopher Marlowe
Doctor Faustus

Christopher Marlowe
Edward II

Arthur Miller
Death of a Salesman

John Milton
Paradise Lost Books I & II

Toni Morrison
Beloved

George Orwell
Nineteen Eighty-Four

Sylvia Plath
Selected Poems

Alexander Pope
Rape of the Lock and other poems

William Shakespeare
Antony and Cleopatra

William Shakespeare
As You Like It

William Shakespeare
Hamlet

William Shakespeare
Henry IV Pt I

William Shakespeare
King Lear

William Shakespeare
Macbeth

William Shakespeare
Measure for Measure

William Shakespeare
The Merchant of Venice

William Shakespeare
A Midsummer Night's Dream

William Shakespeare
Much Ado About Nothing

William Shakespeare
Othello

William Shakespeare
Richard II

William Shakespeare
Richard III

William Shakespeare
Romeo and Juliet

William Shakespeare
The Taming of the Shrew

William Shakespeare
The Tempest

William Shakespeare
Twelfth Night

William Shakespeare
The Winter's Tale

George Bernard Shaw
Saint Joan

Mary Shelley
Frankenstein

Jonathan Swift
Gulliver's Travels and A Modest Proposal

Alfred, Lord Tennyson
Selected Poems

Virgil
The Aeneid

Alice Walker
The Color Purple

Oscar Wilde
The Importance of Being Earnest

Tennessee Williams
A Streetcar Named Desire

Jeanette Winterson
Oranges Are Not the Only Fruit

John Webster
The Duchess of Malfi

Virginia Woolf
To the Lighthouse

W.B. Yeats
Selected Poems

Metaphysical Poets